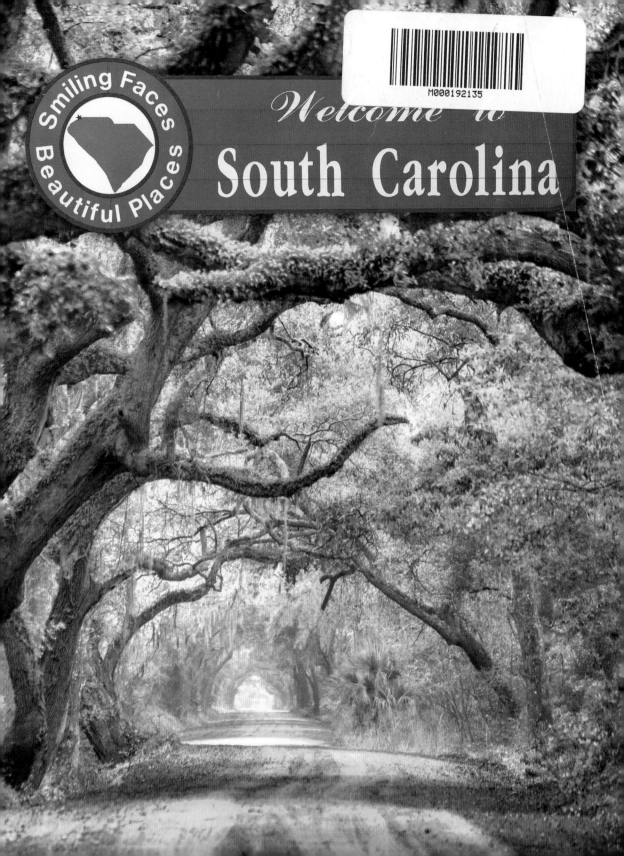

Welcome to **South Carolina**

Smiling Faces Beautiful Places

M000192135

South Carolina
BACK ROAD RESTAURANT
Recipes

A Cookbook & Restaurant Guide

ANITA MUSGROVE

Great American Publishers
www.GreatAmericanPublishers.com
TOLL-FREE 1-888-854-5954

Great American Publishers

171 Lone Pine Church Road • Lena, MS 39094
TOLL-FREE 1-888-854-5954 • www.GreatAmericanPublishers.com

ISBN 978-1-934817-37-7

by Anita Musgrove

10 9 8 7 6 5 4 3 2

Design & Layout: Nichole Stewart
Layout: Zak Simmons
Editorial Assistant: Heather Martin

p22-23: Circa 1913 Shoeless Joe Jackson Fatima Cigarette Premium ©Fatima (Heritage Auctions), via Wikimedia Commons; Ty Cobb & Joe Jackson standing alongside each other, each holding bats ©Library of Congress, via Wikimedia Commons; Shoeless Joe Jackson (r.) of the Chicago White Sox and the New York Yankees' Babe Ruth look at one of Babe's home run bats in 1920 ©New York Daily News, via Wikimedia Commons; Shoeless Joe Jackson, Black Betsy in hand ©Charles M Conlon (Mears Auctions) [Public domain], via Wikimedia Commons • p32-33: Willowbrook Cemetery ©Thompkins Library-Tonya Guy • p46-47: Under bridge, Bridge and creek, Bridge and road ©Greenville County Parks and Recreation • p66-67: Water and rocks; Blue sign; Water spouts ©2010 Ben Truesdale and made available under a Attribution-Noncommercial-Share Alike 2.0 license -- https://www.flickr.com/photos/1f2frfbf/; Church ©Kilodawg06, via Wikimedia Commons • p78-79: EdVenture ©Akhenaton06, via Wikimedia Commons • p92-93: Cotton bale; Horse and cotton ©South Carolina Cotton Museum • p106-107 UFO Welcome Center, Bowman, SC ©mogollon_1 is licensed under CC BY 2.0 https://www.flickr.com/photos/camas/ • p132-133: Mars Bluff Crater ©Kelly Michals • p142-143: Huey Cooper Statue ©alexpalkovich.com; Ronald McNair ©nasacommons -- https://www.flickr.com/photos/nasacommons/; Ronald McNair Statue © Efy96001 via Wikimedia Commons• p150-151: Atalaya and palms; Palm trees and windows ©Ron Osborne, The original uploader was Rono359 at English Wikipedia, via Wikimedia Commons; Atalaya back; Inside courtyard, north side ©Doug Coldwell CC-BY-SA-3.0 (http://creativecommons.org/licenses/by-sa/3.0/)], from Wikimedia Commons • p158-159: Building; Horse; Kitchen table; inside museum ©South Carolina Tobacco Museum • p174-175: Magnolia Plantation House; Purple flowers ©Elisa.rolle, via Wikimedia Commons, Sign; Bridge ©Doug Kerr, via Wikimedia Commons • p208-209: World's Largest Sweet Tea ©Town of Summerville • p222-223: Fort Dorchester ©E. Karl Braun, via Wikimedia Commons; Church ruins ©Lazyksaw, via Wikimedia Commons

Every effort has been made to ensure the accuracy of the information provided in this book.
However, dates, times, and locations are subject to change.
Please call or visit websites for up-to-date information before traveling.

To purchase books in quantity for corporate use, incentives, or fundraising,
please call Great American Publishers at 888-854-5954.

Contents

Welcome to South Carolina

Preface

Are you packed? We are ready to pull out for South Carolina. I have the vehicle gassed up, but my little brown Mercury has been recalled, so she is not able to make the trip this time. No worries, I'm traveling in a rental to the best locally owned restaurants in The Palmetto State. I hope you will journey with me for this 8th edition of the State Back Road Restaurant Recipes Series.

We'll start in the Piedmont Region, located in the upper northwest corner of South Carolina. One of the best locally owned places to dine is **Charlene's Home Cooking**, in the quaint community of Moore. Charlene's serves some of the best soul food ever eaten. Owners Charlene and Mike Davis describe the food served as "cooking from the heart." Charlene uses recipes that have been in her family for generations, like the *Beef Stew* (page 27) she so graciously shared with us.

Need a place to stay while visiting the region? **The Gray House** in Starr is perfect for a nice stay and a delicious meal. The bed and breakfast is in a beautiful, turn-of-the-century home, beside which you can take a romantic stroll to see the gardens and tranquil pond. Try the *Marinated Beef Fillet Tenderloin* (page 43) for a taste of what is in store for your taste buds.

The Whistle Stop at the American Café has the distinction of being the oldest restaurant in the region. Vickie Vernon Hawkins is the third-generation owner of the café. *Miss Vickie's Southern Pecan Pie* (page 51) was handed down to Vickie's mother, Delores Vernon, from her mother, Lillian Style. Now Vickie is sharing it with you. Talk about good.

The first restaurant we'll visit in the Midlands Region, in the center of the state, is **Willie Sue's** in Sumter. Owner Ricky McLeod named his restaurant after his grandmother. Now, there is a grandson any grandmother would be proud to have! The restaurant was constructed using reclaimed wood from Sumter's old railroad station and features historical pictures that recall a simpler time. Enjoy steaks that are cooked to perfection on Ricky's one-of-a-kind wood grill.

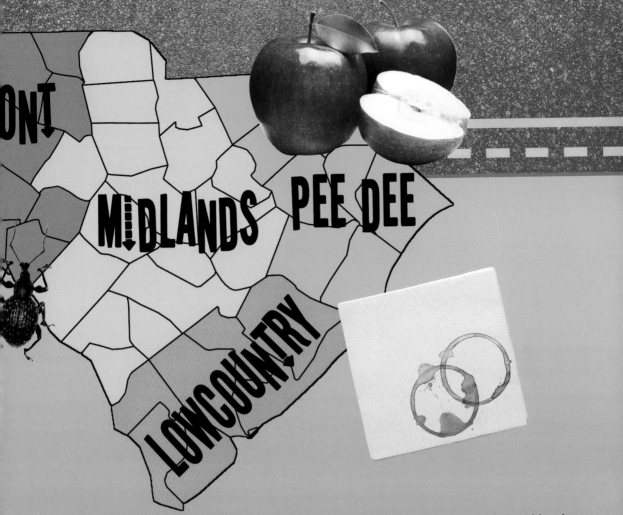

Miller's Bread Basket in Blackville serves home-cooked Amish-Mennonite-style dishes, like their *Shoo-Fly Pie* (page 67). The goal of the owners, Mervin and Anna Miller, is to preserve the theme of fresh, home-cooked meals that have been the staple of the restaurant since it opened in 1987.

Ever wondered where UFOs stop for a bathroom break? (page 102) Did you know there is land that was deeded to Almighty God? (page 64) Are you tired of telling your kids to keep their hands to themselves everywhere you go? (page 76) You'll find all this and more in the Midlands Region of South Carolina.

Now, let's travel to the Pee Dee Region. Love barbecue? **Ball & Que Restaurant** in Georgetown has been known for its 'cue since 1970. Open for breakfast, lunch, and dinner, the rotating menu assures you a wide variety of choices, like cheese biscuits, chicken-fried steak—a favorite of my new traveling partner, Richard Shaw—and, my favorite, chicken and dumplings. Top it off with *Grandma Mildred's Coconut Pie* (page 133), and you are set for the day.

The River's Edge Restaurant in Cheraw invites you to take a seat at their table and enjoy meals just like Mom used to cook. Enjoy favorites like roast beef and meatloaf, and follow up with a large selection of scratch-made desserts that customers describe as "a bit of heaven." Try the *Lemon Icebox Pie* (page 121)—the perfect dessert to end your meal on a sweet note.

Are you an early riser? Then you will enjoy the **Golden Egg Pancake House** in Surfside Beach. The Golden Egg team always delivers on service and taste because they take no shortcuts to make great food. Enjoy their recipe for *Pumpkin Pancakes* (page 157). While you are there, visit **Atalaya Castle** (page 146) and Lake City, which is home to the Bean Market building, a bronze statue of Huey Cooper with his lucky rabbit's foot, and the statue and tomb of Dr. Ronald E. McNair, who died aboard the Space Shuttle *Challenger*. Do you remember where you were when the *Challenger* exploded?

Now, this brings us to the Lowcountry Region. **Angel Oak Restaurant** on Johns Island is a charming eatery serving outstanding Southern-style dishes. Their philosophy is simple—cook with only the freshest ingredients, and present them in a way that best represents the area. Try owner Jay's recipe for *Pimento Cheese Grits* (page 195). Whether served as a side dish or the main dish, it is a guaranteed crowd-pleaser.

As we travel through Walterboro, we'll discover if "country cookin' makes you good lookin'." **Olde House Café** serves down-home American fare, like seafood platters, rib-eye steaks, and delicious country breakfasts. Try their *Potato Casserole* (page 227) and check the mirror. If you don't like what you see, don't call me. At least the food will be good.

Jack's Cosmic Dogs in Mount Pleasant will always be close to my heart. This Alabama girl loves hot dogs. This place is exactly the kind of out-of-the-way, roadside stand my father, Ray Cantrell, and I loved to stop at when traveling together. Dad would have loved some *Jack's Blue Cheese Coleslaw* (page 199) on the five (yes, FIVE!) dogs he always ate. Be sure to visit Jack's Cosmic Dogs, where you'll get the best hot dog around and so much more. While you travel the Lowcountry, don't miss the tree that provides over 17,000 square feet of shade. **Angel Oak** (page 193) is one of the oldest living things in the country. Ownership can be traced back to 1717.

Thank you to all the cookbook collectors, restaurant lovers, and armchair travelers who follow me as I travel to find the best places to stop for a bit while on the road. It is such a joy to discover the foods that these restaurant owners and chefs share. So many times you hear how they learned to cook while working alongside their family—parents, grandparents, aunts, or uncles. There are so many things a person can inherit from their family; one of the best, to me, is the love of cooking.

I still cook pot roasts like my Granny Rice taught me, using the same pot she and my mother, Virginia Cantrell, used for many years. Boy, if I had all the foods that were cooked in that pot, I could open my own restaurant. I would call it Mama Nita's. When the grandkids would ask, "Where are we eating?," my husband, Leonard Musgrove, would answer, "We are going to Mama Nita's." After a while, they figured out we were not going out to eat after all.

I have been very blessed with a wonderful family: my son, Mickey, and his wife, Frankie, who is just another daughter from a different mother; and Sheila and her husband, Roger, who calls me Granny, just like the five grandchildren. My oldest grandchild is Ryan, who is married to Shelbie, and they are parents to my first great-grandson, Trace. Then, there are Nic, Brooke, Morgan, and Bryce. I may not have all the gold in the world, but I do have a lot of silver in my hair and all the love a woman could wish for.

I must also thank my GAP family, where we also stick together through good times and sad times. Sheila and Roger Simmons, the owners, are all about bringing life and the love of Jesus to us all, keeping this family together. From research to unloading books, calling customers to designing pages, each person in our company has had a hand in making this book, and Great American Publishers as a whole, successful. Thank you Brooke, Diane, Nichole, Zak, Heather, Amber, Christy, Tory, Dana, Kimberly, Kori, and Tasha. Hearts and kisses to Richard Shaw, my best bud and traveling partner. Thank you for putting up with me as I stress out over each book.

Thank you for joining me on yet another wonderful adventure. I'll let you know when to pack for North Carolina. We'll be going there soon.

Travel safe and eat hearty,

Anita Musgrove

Anita Musgrove

Let the words of my mouth and the meditation of my heart be acceptable unto thy sight, O LORD, my strength and my redeemer. — Psalm 19:14

Piedmont

GUEST CHECK

DATE	SERVER	TABLE	GUESTS	CHECK NUMBER
				689561

1	Cheese burger	5	49
2	Onion Ring	6	88
1	Chicken Wrap	5	99
		16	36

Thank You - Please Come Again

11

Sullivan's Metropolitan Grill

208 South Main Street, Suite 400
Anderson, SC 29624
864-226-8945
www.sullivansmetrogrill.com • Find us on Facebook

Sullivan's Metropolitan Grill opened in February 1999, born out of the relationship between Chef Bill Nickas and his wife, Chef Sabra Nickas. After graduating Johnson & Wales University, the two worked at eateries throughout South Carolina. With experience under their belts and passion in their hearts, they opened Sullivan's Metropolitan Grill to great success. Today, the full-service, upscale restaurant thrives on classic Southern dishes, like shrimp and grits, and homemade desserts, such as key lime pie and chocolate swirl cheesecake. Stop by for delicious cuisine, beautiful desserts, and the opportunity to help write the Grill's next chapter.

Monday – Friday:
11:00 am to 2:30 pm; 5:30 pm until
Saturday:
5:30 pm until

Raspberry Pecan Brie Vinaigrette

1 (8-ounce) wheel of Brie cheese, softened

½ cup pecans

3 ounces raspberry vinegar

6 ounces Raspberry Monin Syrup

9 ounces canola oil

Salt and pepper to taste

Using a food processor, mix Brie, pecans, vinegar and syrup until smooth. Slowly drizzle in oil. Taste and add salt and pepper to taste. Immediately serve or refrigerate and pull out 20 minutes prior to using.

Restaurant Recipe

Chocolate Chip Cheesecake

Crust:

2 cups ground Oreos

¼ cup melted unsalted butter

Using a large bowl, mix Oreos and butter together. Press crumb mixture into bottom of springform pan; set aside.

Cheesecake:

3 (8-ounce) packages cream cheese, softened

1 cup sugar

3 tablespoons all-purpose flour

½ cup sour cream

3 eggs

1 teaspoon vanilla extract

2 cups chocolate chips, divided

Preheat oven to 350°. Using an electric mixer, mix cream cheese, sugar and flour until smooth. Add sour cream; add eggs, 1 at a time. Add vanilla. Fold in 1½ cups chocolate chips. Pour mixture into prepared crust. Sprinkle remaining chips on top. Bake 1 hour at 350°. Remove from oven, cool to room temperature and refrigerate overnight.

Restaurant Recipe

Broncos Mexican Restaurant

18155 Asheville Highway
Campobello, SC 29322
864-468-4259
Find us on Facebook

Bienvenidos a Broncos Mexican Restaurant. This family-owned restaurant has been serving the Campobello area delicious Mexican fare since it first opened in February 2015. The combination of wonderful food, a comfy atmosphere, and an amazing staff is sure to keep you coming back for more. Occasionally, guests can enjoy live music while they dine, all courtesy of a live band. Come out and experience a taste of Mexico.

Monday – Sunday: 11:00 am to 10:00 pm

Camarones Campechanos

This dish is one of Broncos' best-selling dinner plates. It's very easy to make and over-the-top delicious.

12 jumbo shrimp
1 link chorizo
¼ white onion, thinly sliced
2 to 3 mushrooms, thinly sliced
2 teaspoons canned chipotle

Add all ingredients to a cast-iron skillet over medium heat. Cook 10 to 15 minutes, stirring frequently, until shrimp and chorizo are seared, onion is translucent and mushrooms are tender. Enjoy.

Restaurant Recipe

Fajitas Rio Grande

This is another favorite dish at Broncos, serving up a nice balance of vegetables and meat.

½ cup thinly sliced chicken breast
½ cup thinly sliced steak
Salt and pepper to taste
½ stalk broccoli, chopped
½ stalk cauliflower, chopped
1 bell pepper, seeded and sliced
1 tomato, sliced
¼ white onion, sliced
3 mushrooms, chopped
Flour tortillas

In a cast-iron skillet over medium heat, add chicken, steak, salt and pepper; cook until chicken is no longer pink and steak is no longer red. Stir in remaining ingredients except tortillas. Simmer about 15 minutes until vegetables are tender. Serve in warmed flour tortillas. Enjoy.

Restaurant Recipe

Guacamole Azteca

1 ripe avocado
1 jalapeño pepper
½ white onion
1 tomato
½ sprig fresh cilantro
1 lime
Salt to taste

Dice avocado, jalapeño, onion and tomato; place in a bowl. Mince cilantro and add to bowl with diced ingredients. Squeeze lime into mixture. Add salt to taste. Mix all ingredients until well combined and enjoy with chips. Serves 3 to 4 people.

Restaurant Recipe

Old Edgefield Grill

202 Penn Street
Edgefield, SC 29824
803-637-3222
Find us on Facebook

The Old Edgefield Grill was opened in April 1999 and has been an Edgefield staple ever since. The Grill is housed in a 1906 Queen Victorian home featuring white columnar architecture and crystal chandeliers. A cozy bar with vintage church pews and three dining rooms with antique manteled fireplaces offer a casual yet sophisticated atmosphere. Guests will enjoy a variety of dishes, like salads, burgers, sandwiches, and fried baskets. Try the shrimp and grits, or a juicy pan-roasted duck breast. Visit the Old Edgefield Grill for Southern comfort dining, hospitality, culture, and delicious cuisine.

Tuesday: 11:00 am to 2:00 pm
Wednesday – Saturday:
11:00 am to 2:00 pm; 5:00 pm to 9:00 pm

Old Edgefield Shrimp & Grits with Fried Onion Hay

1 cup uncooked yellow stone-ground grits (not instant)

1 cup heavy cream

2 tablespoons butter

Salt and pepper to taste

Oil for frying

1 large yellow onion, cut into ⅛-inch slices

2 cups all-purpose flour

½ cup unsalted butter, softened

2 pounds raw, tail-on Black Tiger shrimp, peeled and deveined

3 pounds fresh Roma tomatoes, large dice

¼ cup medium diced onion

¾ cup diced andouille sausage

¼ cup Chef Paul Prudhomme's blackened seasoning

1 cup dry white wine

In a medium saucepan over high heat, bring 4 cups water to a boil. Whisk in grits, stirring constantly until they begin to bubble; set to low heat and simmer, regularly whisking, about 1 hour or until thickened. Whisk in cream, butter, salt and pepper; cook over low heat until grits are tender and thick as pudding. Remove from heat, keeping warm in a slow cooker. In another saucepan, preheat 4 inches oil to 350°. Dredge onion slices in flour until evenly coated and broken apart; shake off excess flour and fry 3 to 5 minutes, or until golden brown. Remove Onion Hay from oil and drain on a paper towel; sprinkle with salt and set aside. In a large skillet over high heat, melt unsalted butter; add shrimp, tomatoes, onion, sausage and blackened seasoning, sweating until shrimp are pink and heated through. Remove from heat and deglaze pan with wine, stirring in 5 tablespoons water. Spoon grits into a serving bowl; top with shrimp sauce and Onion Hay. Enjoy.

Restaurant Recipe

Carolina Barbecue Shack

728 Montague Avenue
Greenwood, SC 29649
864-223-2202
www.carolinabbqshack.com • Find us on Facebook

When Burgess Mauldin was a child, her parents held big family gatherings at their farm every Easter. Part of the family tradition was to roast a pig over an open fire in a hand-dug pit. The meat was delicious. Years later, when her father retired from thirty years in education, he opened up Carolina Barbecue Shack slightly off the beaten path in Greenwood. Guests will enjoy a wide variety of barbecue classics slow-smoked over twenty-four hours on a custom-made, sixteen-foot smoker. They also make the best hash in the state. Stop by for South Carolina barbecue at its finest.

Wednesday: 11:00 am to 4:00 pm
Thursday – Saturday: 11:00 am to 6:00 pm

Banana Pudding

8 bananas, sliced
1 (11-ounce) box vanilla wafers
1 (112-ounce) can vanilla pudding
2 (8-ounce) containers Cool Whip

Layer bananas, wafers and pudding. Spread Cool Whip over top. Refrigerate at least 1 hour before serving.

Restaurant Recipe

Carolina Caviar

1 (15.5-ounce) can black-eyed peas
1 (11-ounce) can Mexicorn
3 Roma tomatoes, seeded and chopped
1 small onion, chopped
1 cup hot picante sauce
¼ cup chopped fresh cilantro
2 garlic cloves, minced
2 tablespoons fresh lime juice

Rinse and drain peas and corn. In a large bowl, mix all ingredients. Cover and chill at least 2 hours. Serve with tortilla chips.

Restaurant Recipe

Potato & Onion Casserole

6 cups sliced red potato
6 cups sliced Vidalia onions+
1 stick butter, sliced into pats
Dry rub, salt and pepper
2 cups shredded Swiss cheese

Preheat oven to 350°. Layer 3 cups potatoes, 3 cups onions and dot with butter. Season with dry rub, salt and pepper to taste. Repeat layering and top with cheese. Cover with aluminum foil and bake 30 minutes. Uncover and bake 30 more minutes.

Restaurant Recipe

WHY IS HE CALLED SHOELESS JOE?

If you don't know his history, the name "Shoeless Joe Jackson" may conjure images of someone who walks around barefoot all the time. In actuality, Joseph Jefferson Jackson—one of baseball's greatest natural hitters of all time—ran the bases only once in his stocking feet.

In 1908, Joe was playing semi-pro ball with the Greenville Spinners, and his new shoes were causing painful blisters on his feet. For the second game, he removed his shoes before going up to bat. After hitting a triple in the 7th inning, a fan of the opposing team shouted, "You shoeless son-of-a-gun!" The name "Shoeless Joe" stuck.

Joe's parents, George and Martha Jackson, had six children and very little money. When Joe was just six years old, he worked at a local mill, sweeping cotton dust off the wooden floors. In 1901, the family moved to West Greenville, where Joe went to work at Brandon Mill to help his family. Working 12 hours shifts did not afford the luxury of school, so Joe was uneducated and unable to read or write.

He was, however, chosen for the Brandon Mill men's baseball team. His play was so exceptional that he became a hometown celebrity. Joe's home runs were known as "Saturday Specials," his line drives "Blue Darters," and his glove, "A place where triples go to die."

In 1908, Joe signed with the professional league. After working his way up to the big league playing for Cleveland, he batted .408 in 1911—the highest batting average ever recorded by a rookie. He set many more records during his career.

In August 1915, he was traded to the Chicago White Sox for $31,500 cash and three players. The White Sox were a talented team, winning the world championship in 1917 and the American League pennant in 1919. They were the heavy favorites to beat Cincinnati in the 1919 World Series but lost to the Reds. In response to suspicions that the White Sox were under the influence of sports bookies, Joe Jackson and seven other White Sox players were accused of conspiring to throw the 1919 World Series and banned from playing professional baseball.

Joe Jackson proclaimed himself innocent until the day he died, pointing out that his performance in the 1919 World Series would stand against the performance of any other man in that series or all the ones before. His supporters are quick to point out that Joe played an outstanding game, hitting .375 for the Series, the highest on either team. He had twelve hits (a tie for the World Series record at the time); six RBIs and no errors in eight games. He accounted for eleven of twenty runs by the Sox and hit the only home run in the Series.

Despite his banishment from professional baseball, Joe Jackson continues to be one of the most beloved and publicized ballplayers of all time. He is a local hero in Greenville, where Jackson is memorialized with a life-size statue of himself, created by South Carolina sculptor Doug Young. Joe's original home is now the Shoeless Joe Jackson Museum. The address is 356 Field Street, in honor of his lifetime batting average.

Joseph Jefferson Jackson "Shoeless Joe"

1888 - 1951
Lifetime Batting Average: .356
(third highest in baseball history)

Shoeless Joe Jackson Statue

Fluor Field
945 South Main Street
Greenville, SC 29601

Shoeless Joe Jackson Museum

356 Field Street
Greenville, SC 29601
www.shoelessjoejackson.org

DELIGHTFUL DISHES
Restaurant & Catering

13144 Asheville Highway
Inman, SC 29349
864-472-6305
Find us on Facebook

Delightful Dishes opened in January 1997 and has been serving the Inman area as a restaurant and catering business ever since. At Delightful Dishes, you'll find everything from their famous chicken salad to delectable sweets. Need a family dinner without the hassle of prep? Pick up a frozen casserole, like lasagna, chicken pot pie, or mac and cheese. You can also stop in five days a week for daily lunch plates, house-made sandwiches, salads, and delicious homemade desserts. If you'd like a cake for a special occasion, they offer many varieties, including pound cake, strawberry cake, and peanut butter fudge. Stop by Delightful Dishes, and get your dish on.

Catering:
Monday – Friday: 9:00 am to 4:30 pm
Lunch:
Monday – Friday: 11:00 am to 2:00 pm

No-Bake Chocolate Oatmeal Cookies

¼ cup cocoa

2 cups sugar

½ cup milk

1 stick butter

2½ cups oats

½ cup peanut butter

1 teaspoon vanilla extract

Combine cocoa and sugar in a saucepan over medium heat. Add milk and butter and bring mixture to boil. Boil 2 minutes; remove from heat. Stir in remaining ingredients. Spoon mixture onto a cookie sheet lined with wax paper. Cool completely before serving. Enjoy.

Restaurant Recipe

Chicken Pecan Quiche

1 cup all-purpose flour

1⅓ cups shredded Cheddar cheese, divided

1 cup chopped pecans, divided

½ teaspoon salt

¼ teaspoon paprika

⅓ cup vegetable oil

Filling:

1 cup sour cream

½ cup chicken stock

¼ cup mayonnaise

3 eggs, lightly beaten

⅓ cup shredded Swiss cheese

¼ cup minced onion

3 drops hot sauce

2 cups cooked, finely chopped chicken

Preheat oven to 350°. In a medium bowl, combine flour, 1 cup Cheddar, ¾ cup pecans, salt and paprika; stir well. Stir in oil. Firmly press mixture into bottom and up sides of a 9-inch deep-dish pie pan. Bake 12 minutes. Cool completely. Meanwhile, make filling. In a bowl, whisk together sour cream, chicken stock, mayonnaise and eggs until smooth. Stir in Swiss, remaining Cheddar, onion, remaining pecans and hot sauce; set aside. Spread chicken over bottom of cooled crust. Pour liquid mixture over chicken. Place on cookie sheet and bake at 350° for 55 minutes or until set. Let stand 10 minutes before serving. Enjoy.

Restaurant Recipe

Blue Collar Bistro

507 Church Street
Johnston, SC 29832
803-275-4500
www.thebluecollarbistro.net • Find us on Facebook

Blue Collar Bistro is a casual dining restaurant in Johnston featuring a diverse menu of Southern cuisine prepared from fresh ingredients. From the Blue Collar Ribs & Wings to the homemade Macaroni & Cheese, you'll find something to please everyone in your party. Sample the daily menu and specials. On Tuesdays evenings, have breakfast for dinner from the breakfast buffet. Wednesday through Saturday you can dig in at the all-you-can-eat buffet. Close out the week with the famous Sunday buffet, loaded down with a wide variety of fine, down-home cuisine. Stop by Blue Collar Bistro and taste the difference.

Tuesday: 5:00 pm to 8:00 pm
Wednesday – Saturday: 11:30 am to 8:00 pm
Sunday: 11:00 am to 5:00 pm

Blue Collar Bistro

Taste the Difference!

Blue Collar Brown Rice Casserole

½ stick butter
1 small onion, diced
1 cup uncooked rice
1 (10.5-ounce) can beef consommé
1 (4.5-ounce) jar mushrooms

Preheat oven to 350°. In a medium saucepan over medium heat, add butter, onion and rice; brown until onions are tender and rice is slightly browned. Remove from heat and pour into a 9x9-inch baking pan. Pour in beef consommé and top with mushrooms. Bake 25 to 30 minutes, or until rice is browned and fully cooked. Makes a great side dish with beef or pork.

Restaurant Recipe

Tomato Pie

2 large tomatoes
1 deep-dish pie crust
1 small onion, diced
Salt and pepper to taste
½ cup mayonnaise
½ cup sour cream
1 cup shredded Cheddar cheese, divided
1 tablespoon chopped sweet basil, divided

Preheat oven to 350°. Slice tomatoes and put into pie shell; top with diced onion. Sprinkle with salt and pepper. In a large bowl, mix mayonnaise, sour cream, ½ cup Cheddar and ½ tablespoon basil; spread mixture evenly over top of tomatoes and onions. Top with remaining Cheddar and basil. Bake 25 minutes, or until bubbly and brown. Makes a great side dish or try it for breakfast or brunch. Enjoy.

Restaurant Recipe

Charlene's Home Cooking

1136 East Blackstock Road
Moore, SC 29369
864-764-1111
www.charleneshomecooking.com • Find us on Facebook

Located in the quaint community of Moore, Charlene's Home Cooking offers up the best soul food in the South. Opened by owners Charlene and Mike Davis in February 2010, this homey restaurant generously serves up "cooking from the heart" using recipes that have been in Charlene's family for generations. Carrying on the traditions of the family matriarch Annie Laura Sims-Alexander, whom everyone affectionately called "Ma Bessie" or "Ma Bess" for short, Charlene's Home Cooking is the go-to place when craving a home-cooked meal. Whenever you're feeling nostalgic or just hungry, wander on in to Charlene's Home Cooking where everyone is treated like family.

Monday & Thursday: 11:00 am to 6:00 pm
Friday & Sunday: 11:00 am to 7:00 pm
Saturday: 10:30 am to 6:00 pm

Charlene's Beef Stew

5 pounds beef stew meat

5 tablespoons meat tenderizer

2 pounds red potatoes, quartered

**2 large yellow onions, chopped
into ½-inch pieces**

**1 pound carrots, chopped
into 1-inch pieces**

**1 pound celery, chopped
into ½-inch pieces**

½ cup roast beef seasoning blend

½ cup chicken seasoning blend

3 tablespoons kosher salt

1 teaspoon crushed red pepper

3 bay leaves

1 cup poultry gravy mix

1 cup brown gravy mix

Preheat oven to 350°. In a bowl, mix meat with tenderizer; set aside. In a large roasting pan, mix together vegetables, seasoning blends, salt, pepper and bay leaves; mix in meat and cover with water. Bake 3 to 3½ hours, or until meat is tender. Remove from oven and strain, reserving broth; return meat and vegetable mixture to roasting pan and set aside. In a large saucepan, add 1 cup cold water to gravy mixes; stir in 2 cups reserved broth (or more if a thinner gravy is desired). Bring gravy to a low simmer, stirring constantly until thickened; pour over top of meat and vegetable mixture. Bake 30 minutes more. Serve over rice.

Restaurant Recipe

Old-Fashioned Fudge

1½ cups sugar
¼ cup white Karo syrup
4 tablespoons cocoa powder
½ cup milk
Pinch salt
1 stick margarine
1 teaspoon vanilla
1 tablespoon peanut butter, optional

In a cast-iron skillet over medium high heat, mix together sugar, Karo, cocoa, milk and salt. Cook about 10 minutes, stirring constantly until mixture reaches soft-ball stage on candy thermometer (235°); remove from heat. Add margarine, vanilla and peanut butter. Let sit, without disturbing, until margarine melts. Whisk until mixture loses its gloss and starts to thicken. Pour into a buttered dish; set aside until cooled. Cut into squares and enjoy.

Local Favorite

Bacon Wrapped Little Smokies

1 (12-ounce) package sliced bacon
1 (16-ounce) package Little Smokies
2 cups brown sugar
Honey
Wooden toothpicks

Preheat oven to 350°. Cut each bacon slice into 3 equal lengths. Wrap 1 piece of bacon around each Little Smokie; skewer with a toothpick. Place in a baking dish, sprinkle with brown sugar and top with honey to taste. Cook 30 minutes, flip and cook 30 more minutes or until bacon is crisp on both sides. Serve while still hot.

Local Favorite

Company Burger Casserole

3 tablespoons vegetable oil
1 medium onion, chopped
2 cloves garlic, chopped
1 pound ground chuck
8 whole sun-dried tomatoes, packed in oil, drained and minced
1 (28-ounce) can crushed tomatoes
2 tablespoons oregano
2 teaspoons dried marjoram
Salt and pepper to taste
1 (16-ounce) package ziti
2 large eggs
⅔ cup whipping cream
2 cups shredded mozzarella, divided
3 tablespoons freshly grated Parmesan cheese

Preheat oven to 350°. Heat oil in skillet over medium high heat. Add onion and garlic; sauté 5 minutes. Stir in ground meat, cooking until no longer pink. Add all tomato products and seasonings; simmer 15 minutes while you cook ziti in a large pot of salted water until al dente. Drain pasta. Using a 3-quart Dutch oven whisk together eggs and cream. Quickly toss ziti into cream mixture. Add meat mixture, stirring to combine. Fold in 1½ cups mozzarella. Top pasta mixture with remaining cheeses. Bake uncovered for 30 to 40 minutes or until cheese is melted and bubbling. Serve at once with garlic bread and a nice green salad.

Local Favorite

Melting Moments Cookies

1 cup flour
½ cup cornstarch
½ cup powdered sugar
¾ cup margarine
1 teaspoon vanilla

Using a bowl, mix together flour, cornstarch and sugar; set aside. In a mixing bowl, beat margarine with an electric mixer until smooth. Slowly beat in flour mixture and vanilla until well blended. Cover and refrigerate 1 hour. Preheat oven to 375°. Shape dough into 1-inch balls and place on ungreased cookie sheet 1½ inches apart. Flatten slightly with lightly floured fork. Bake 10 to 12 minutes or until edges are lightly browned. Makes 3 dozen cookies.

Local Favorite

GRAVE OR TRAP DOOR?

The answer is yes. Willowbrook Cemetery, the second most historic cemetery in South Carolina, is home to the final resting place of Dr. James Adams DeVore. Before his death in 1895, Dr. Devore was a very eccentric character. According to local legend, the trap door on top of his grave covers a tunnel with an arched entrance that leads to Dr. Devore himself, sitting in a chair behind glass.

The oldest marked grave in the cemetery is dated 1820. There are soldiers buried there from every major war fought by the United States—the American Revolution, War of 1812, Second Seminole War, Mexican War, American Civil War, Spanish-American War, World War I, World War II, Korea, and Vietnam. Many politicians are buried there also, including Strom Thurmond as well as other governors, senators, members of the House of Representatives, and 150 Confederate soldiers (including four brigadier generals of the Confederacy).

Some interesting people interred at Willowbrook include Lucy Holcomb Pickens, the "Queen of the Confederacy"; Matthew Calbraith Butler, a Confederate major general during the Civil War who had his embalmed foot that he lost years earlier buried with him; and Reverend John Lake, a missionary to China whose grave is marked with a stone from the leper colony he started.

The sweetest testimony from Willowbrook is a touching love story. Physician Elbert Bland and his wife, Rebecca, are buried in a single grave. In 1863, Dr. Bland died due to injuries suffered in the Battle of Chickamauga. When Rebecca died in 1891, she asked that her husband's grave and coffin be opened and her body placed on top of his, so they could rest together forever.

Willowbrook Cemetery is a peaceful and beautiful place to spend a day immersed in history.

Willowbrook Cemetery

212 Church Street
Edgefield, SC 29824
803-637-4010

Shrimp Kedgeree

1 tablespoon canola or peanut oil
1 tablespoon butter
1 red onion, diced
2 carrots, sliced into thin coins or diced
1½ cups long grain rice
1 tablespoon curry powder
2 tablespoons minced garlic
3 cups vegetable broth (or a mix of vegetable/chicken broth)
Salt and pepper to taste
½ cup butter beans
1 pound shrimp, peeled and deveined
Juice and zest from 1 lemon
4 hard-boiled eggs, peeled and quartered
1 to 2 tablespoons chopped fresh cilantro

Heat oil in a large saucepan, over medium heat; add butter. When hot, add onion and carrots; cook until tender. Add rice, garlic and curry powder; stir well. Cook about 2 minutes, allowing rice to toast. Add broth and bring to a boil, reduce heat and cover. Simmer 20 minutes or until tender. Taste and add salt and black pepper. Add butter beans, shrimp, lemon zest and juice; stir well. Cover and steam 5 minutes. Place in a serving bowl and garnish with quartered eggs and cilantro.

Local Favorite

Hot Apple Soup

4 Granny Smith apples
4 McIntosh apples
2 tablespoons lemon juice
¼ teaspoon nutmeg
½ teaspoon cinnamon
1 cup light cream or half-and-half
Unsweetened whipped cream for garnish

Peel, core and quarter apples. In a saucepan, combine apples, 2½ cups water, lemon juice, nutmeg and cinnamon. Bring to a boil and simmer 15 minutes or until apples are soft. Using an immersion blender, puree soup. Add cream and heat through; do not boil. Garnish each serving with a dollop of whipped cream.

Local Favorite

Super Quick Dinner Rolls

1 cup self-rising flour
½ cup milk
2 tablespoons mayonnaise

Preheat oven to 350°. If not already using a nonstick muffin pan, grease five cups of a regular muffin pan with nonstick spray. In a medium bowl, mix all ingredients until combined. Divide batter evenly into prepared muffin cups. Bake 15 minutes or until nicely puffed and browned.

Local Favorite

Hot Tamale Dip

1 (15-ounce) can chili without beans
1 (10-ounce) can Ro-Tel tomatoes
2 (15-ounce) cans tamales, mashed
1 pound cheese, cubed
Fritos

Combine all ingredients in a slow cooker and simmer stirring occasionally until melted. Serve with Fritos.

Local Favorite

Old Fashioned Squash Casserole

10 cups sliced yellow squash
1½ cups chopped sweet onion
3 cups chicken broth
1 cup shredded Cheddar cheese, divided
½ cup sour cream
½ cup mayonnaise
2 tablespoons unsalted butter, divided
1 teaspoon salt
½ teaspoon ground black pepper
¼ teaspoon garlic powder
1 large egg, lightly beaten
1½ cups crushed buttery round crackers, divided
3 cups water

Preheat oven to 350°. Spray a 2-quart baking dish with nonstick cooking spray; set aside. In a Dutch oven, bring squash, onion, 3 cups water and broth to a boil. Reduce heat to medium-low; simmer until squash is crisp tender, approximately 7 minutes. Drain well. In a large bowl, gently stir together squash mixture, ½ cup cheese, sour cream, mayonnaise, 1 tablespoon butter, salt, pepper, garlic powder and egg. Spoon half the squash mixture into prepared dish, spreading evenly. Sprinkle with with half the crushed crackers. Top with remaining squash mixture, remaining crackers, and remaining cheese. Dot with remaining butter. Bake 25 minutes or until cheese melts.

Local Favorite

Boots' & Sonny's Drive-In

120 East Henry Street
Spartanburg, SC 29306
864-582-2439
www.bootsandsonnys.com • Find us on Facebook

Welcome to the Home of the Hot Dog Man. Boots' & Sonny's Drive-In is a third-generation family eatery renowned for serving its family's chili recipe. The Drive-In's famous chili is slow simmered and made fresh every day beginning at 5 in the morning, and it makes a great topping on everything from hot dogs and burgers to French fries and more. From veggie soup to onion rings to homemade chili, this family-owned traditional diner has stayed true to its roots, and it's these fresh-made features that keep patrons coming back for more.

Monday – Friday: 10:00 am to 8:00 pm

What do we recommend? Our #1 Best Seller: Two hot dogs with homemade chili, chili cheese fries and a drink.

Bubba's BBQ & Bash

827 West Blackstock Road
Spartanburg, SC 29301
864-582-7487
www.bubbasbbqbash.com • Find us on Facebook

Since 2002, Bubba's BBQ & Bash has been serving simple and satisfying barbecue, sandwiches, soups, salads, and so much more. Bubba's is the only barbecue place around that does it the old-fashioned way—with fire! You can also enjoy beefed-up burgers and shakes so big and bad that you'll be coming back for more. Bubba's even won Spartanburg's Best of the Best People's Choice Award in both 2017 and 2018. Adjacent to Bubba's is Carolina Culinary Creations, a catering business featuring a diverse menu and staff equipped to handle all special occasions, from family reunions to weddings. Stop by Bubba's BBQ & Bash, the hottest BBQ Bash in town, and enjoy some good mood food for the whole family.

Monday – Saturday: 11:00 am to 8:00 pm

SPARTANBURG'S OFFICIAL COMMUNITY CHOICE AWARDS
★2018★
BEST OF THE
best
SPARTANBURG
Herald-Journal
GoUpstate.com
SPARTANBURG'S OFFICIAL COMMUNITY CHOICE AWARDS

Peach Cobbler

2 cups white sugar
2 sticks butter, melted
1 tablespoon vanilla extract
3 cups milk
2 cups self-rising flour
1 (32-ounce) can peaches, drained
Brown sugar for topping

Preheat oven to 350°. In a bowl, whisk together sugar, butter, vanilla and milk. Gradually stir in flour until smooth; pour into a buttered 9x13-inch baking dish. Mix in peaches and sprinkle top with brown sugar. Bake 45 minutes or until golden brown.

Restaurant Recipe

Southern Slaw

5 pounds cabbage
¼ cup white vinegar
½ cup diced onions
1½ cups sugar
4 cups mayonnaise

Rinse cabbage thoroughly, then pat dry. Remove and discard outermost leaves and cut bottom of stem off. Finely chop cabbage and add to a large bowl; set aside. In another large bowl, mix together all ingredients, except cabbage, until smooth. Fold in cabbage until well combined. Refrigerate several hours before serving. Enjoy.

Restaurant Recipe

Deviled Oysters

1 quart whole oysters, drained
½ cup melted butter
2 lemons, juiced
1 teaspoon red pepper flakes
2 large eggs
3 cups breadcrumbs
Oil for frying

Lay oysters on paper towels to dry. In a low dish, mix butter, lemon juice and pepper flakes. Place oysters in butter mixture and marinate 1 hour. In a small bowl, beat eggs. In another bowl, place breadcrumbs. Dip each oyster in breadcrumbs, then egg and back in breadcrumbs; set on wire rack until ready to fry. Heat oil in saucepan to 325°. Drop in a few oysters at a time, taking care not to overcrowd. Fry until golden brown.

Local Favorite

Best Ever Chocolate Pie

3 eggs, separated
1 cup milk
1 cup sugar
2 tablespoons cocoa
2 tablespoons flour
2 tablespoons butter
½ teaspoon vanilla extract
1 pie shell, partially baked

Beat egg yolks with milk, reserving whites for meringue; set aside. Mix sugar, cocoa and flour; set aside. Using a large iron skillet over medium heat, melt butter. Add sugar mixture; mix well. Add egg mixture, stirring constantly. Increase heat until filling begins to thicken, then decrease heat. Continue to cook over low heat, stirring constantly, until very thick. Remove from heat; stir in vanilla. Pour into pie shell.

Meringue:

3 egg whites
3 tablespoons sugar
½ teaspoon vanilla extract

Preheat oven to 350°. Beat egg whites while gradually adding sugar until stiff but not dry. Beat in vanilla. Spread over pie, making sure to seal edges. Bake 10 to 15 minutes or until brown.

Local Favorite

Griddle Cakes

2 cups flour
¼ cup sugar
½ teaspoon salt
1½ teaspoons baking powder
2 eggs
1½ cups milk
4 tablespoons butter, melted

Preheat flat griddle. In a bowl, sift together flour, sugar, salt and baking powder. In another bowl, beat eggs and milk together. Mix flour mixture into egg mixture and add butter. Test temperature of griddle by sprinkling a few drops of water on surface. If water seems to dance about then evaporate, griddle is hot enough. Drop batter on griddle by ½ cupsful. Brown one side before flipping over to brown other side. Serve with butter on top and drizzle with syrup.

Local Favorite

Granny Pie Crust

2½ cups all-purpose flour
1 heaping teaspoon baking powder
Pinch salt
1 cup cold butter
1 cup pure lard
½ cup ice water

In a bowl, sift flour, baking powder and salt. Cut butter and lard into flour mixture with 2 knives. Mix in just enough water to form a stiff dough. Refrigerate 30 minutes. Remove from refrigerator, divide in half and roll out on a floured surface to desired thickness. Repeat with other half of dough. Makes enough dough for 2 crusts.

Local Favorite

Ike's Korner Grill

104 Archer Road
Spartanburg, SC 29303
864-542-0911
www.restaurantwebx.com/IkesKornerGrill • Find us on Facebook

Opened in 1954, Ike's Korner Grill has been serving the Spartanburg area for over sixty years. This lively, family-owned joint is famous for its burgers, which are widely considered to be the best around. If you're feeling up to it, take on the Ike's Wall of Fame Burger Challenge. Finish the entire four-patty tower of bacon, bologna, fried eggs, chili, and fixings in forty-five minutes, and you'll receive a T-shirt, your photo on the wall, and the burger for free. Ike's also serves plate lunches, salads, sandwiches, hotdogs, onion rings, fries, and beers. Visit Ike's today for delicious food in unfussy digs.

Tuesday – Friday: 10:00 am to 9:00 pm
Saturday: 10:00 am to 3:00 pm

Swiss Steak

½ cup flour
1 (2-pound) package cube steaks
¼ cup oil
½ onion, chopped
½ bell pepper, chopped
2 cups tomato juice
Salt and black pepper to taste

Preheat oven to 300°. On a clean surface, pound flour into both sides of steaks by hand. Add oil to skillet over medium heat; brown steaks. Transfer steaks to a 9x13-inch casserole dish; add onion, pepper, tomato juice, salt and black pepper. Cover and bake 1½ to 2 hours.

Local Favorite

The Gray House

111 Stone's Throw Avenue
Starr, SC 29684
864-352-6778
www.thegrayhousesc.com • Find us on Facebook

Nestled in the rolling foothills of Upstate South Carolina, The Gray House is the perfect destination for fine dining and restful relaxation. This turn-of-the-century home houses a full-service restaurant featuring traditional Southern fare. It's also a quaint bed-and-breakfast that makes for a perfect romantic getaway. You'll fall in love with the mouth-watering meals, beautifully appointed suites, well-manicured gardens, and the tranquil pond. The Gray House is a popular spot for weddings and other events, and offers both on-site and off-premises catering. Visit The Gray House today.

Lunch:
Tuesday – Friday & Sunday: 11:00 am to 2:00 pm
Dinner:
Friday & Saturday: 5:00 pm until

Marinated Beef Fillet Tenderloin

1 (7-ounce) can tomato paste
1½ cups water
2 tablespoons prepared mustard
½ tablespoon Worcestershire sauce
2 (0.7-ounce) envelopes Italian salad dressing mix
1 (5- to 6-pound) beef fillet tenderloin

Combine all ingredients except meat; stir well. Pierce meat in several places. Place marinade and meat in a heavy-duty zip-close plastic bag; refrigerate 8 hours. Preheat oven to 425°. Remove meat, reserving marinade; place on a roasting pan. Place marinade in a saucepan over medium heat; bring to a boil for 2 minutes. Bake 30 to 45 minutes, basting occasionally with remaining marinade. Makes 12 to 14 servings.

Restaurant Recipe

WHERE DO YOU FIND SOUTH CAROLINA'S LAST COVERED BRIDGE?

Campbell's Covered Bridge is a wooden, covered bridge that crosses Beaverdam Creek in northeastern Greenville County, near the small town of Gowensville.

Constructed in 1909, Campbell's Covered Bridge is the last remaining covered bridge in South Carolina. This beautiful structure is 38 feet long by 12 feet wide. It was constructed by Charles Irwin Willis in the relatively rare four-span, Howe truss design and features vertical iron rods and diagonal pine timbers.

In the early 1900s, there were several towns clustered on either side of Beaverdam Creek. Before construction of the bridge, it could take up to a full day to travel all the way upstream or downstream to another bridge just to get over to the communities on the other side. Campbell's Covered Bridge cut he commute time down to just around an hour.

The bridge is named for Alexander Lafayette Campbell (1836–1920), who built and maintained a nearby grist mill for many years. It was restored in 1964 by the Crescent Garden Club, then again in 1990.

Greenville County closed the bridge to motorized traffic in the early 1980s. In 2005, Sylvia Pittman sold ten acres of land surrounding the bridge to Greenville County. The bridge, along with that land, is now a park where you can picnic, explore the remaining foundations of the old mill and home site, wet your feet in Beaverdam Creek, and learn about the area through interpretive signage.

Campbell's Covered Bridge was added to the National Register of Historic Places on July 1, 2009.

Campbell's Covered Bridge

171 Campbell Covered Bridge Road
Landrum, SC 29356

Managed by: Greenville County Parks and Recreation
4806 Old Spartanburg Road
Taylors, SC 29687
864-288-6470
www.greenvillecounty.org

Upcountry Provisions

6809 State Park Road
Travelers Rest, SC 29690
864-834-8433
www.upcountryprovisions.com • Find us on Facebook

Upcountry Provisions opened in March 2012, bringing with it a menu of fresh-made options to the Travelers Rest community. Each dish is prepared using fresh ingredients, like local and organic lettuce, local milk, and local eggs. The selection of breakfast breads, pastries, pies, cakes, and bistro items vary according to season, availability, and the chef's fancy. Enjoy locally roasted coffee or a freshly brewed cup of artisanal tea. The restaurant is also dog friendly for patrons with furry friends. Stop by for a delicious sandwich, fresh-baked bread, and a picnic in the Grove, a rustic outdoor venue featuring their community music series.

Monday – Thursday: 7:30 am to 7:00 pm
Friday & Saturday: 7:30 am to 8:00 pm

Warm Bacon Salad

6 slices bacon, cooked
¼ cup cranberry chutney
¼ cup feta
1 quart salad greens
2 tablespoon Curried Pecans
Balsamic dressing to taste

Preheat oven to 400°. On a baking sheet, place bacon, chutney and feta; bake 5 minutes, or until bacon is crispy. Remove from oven and chop bacon. In a medium mixing bowl, add salad greens; top with bacon, chutney and feta. Add curried pecans and toss together. Add balsamic dressing around the perimeter of bowl and lightly toss to dress. Yields 4 side salads or 2 entrée salads. Serve and enjoy.

Restaurant Recipe

Curried Pecans

6 cups pecans
1 tablespoon oil
½ cup sugar
2 teaspoons curry
1 pinch cayenne
½ teaspoon salt

Preheat oven to 400°. In a large bowl, toss pecans in oil until lightly coated. Add dry ingredients and toss until evenly coated. Spread pecans in a single layer over a cookie sheet. Bake 5 to 8 minutes, or until toasted. Cool completely and store in an airtight container.

Restaurant Recipe

Southern Broccoli Casserole

6 cups fresh broccoli florets
1 (10.74-ounce) can cream
of mushroom soup
1 cup mayonnaise
½ stick butter
2 eggs
½ medium onion, finely chopped
¼ teaspoon black pepper
½ teaspoon salt
1½ cups shredded sharp Cheddar cheese
1 sleeve buttery round
crackers, finely crushed

Place broccoli in steamer basket over simmering water. Cover and steam for approximately 5 minutes. Chop into bite-sized pieces. Preheat oven to 350°. In a large bowl, combine broccoli, soup, mayonnaise, butter, eggs, onion, salt and pepper. Mix well; add 1 cup cheese and mix again. Place mixture in buttered casserole dish. Top with remaining cheese and crushed crackers. Bake 30 to 40 minutes and let stand 15 minutes before serving.

Local Favorite

Easy Nachos

1 (16-ounce) bag corn chips,
Doritos or Tostitos
1 (8-ounce) can refried beans
½ pound Monterey Jack cheese,
sliced or grated
1 (6-ounce) jar pickled sliced jalapeño
peppers, drained
1 (4-ounce) can sliced black
olives, drained

Preheat oven to 300°. Scatter chips on a baking sheet. Spoon refried beans over chips; drape cheese slices over top. Scatter peppers and olives over top. Bake 5 to 10 minutes or until cheese is melted and nachos are hot.

Local Favorite

Sweet Potato Crab Soup

4 tablespoons butter, divided
2 medium shallots, finely chopped
3 garlic cloves, minced
4 cups peeled, cubed sweet potatoes
1 teaspoon salt, divided
½ teaspoon ground cinnamon
½ teaspoon cayenne pepper
5 cups vegetable stock
2 cups heavy whipping cream
4 teaspoons fresh thyme leaves, divided
12 ounces lump crabmeat, drained
Croutons

In a Dutch Oven over medium heat, melt 2 tablespoons butter; sauté shallots and garlic until tender. Stir in potatoes, 3/4 teaspoon salt, cinnamon, cayenne and stock; bring to a boil. Reduce heat and simmer 15 minutes. Puree soup using an immersion blender or cool slightly and puree in blender; return to pan. Stir in cream and 2 teaspoons thyme; bring to a boil. Reduce heat and simmer uncovered 5 minutes. Meanwhile in a large skillet over medium heat, melt remaining butter. Add crab with remaining salt and thyme; cook 5 minutes, stirring gently to combine. Serve soup in a bowl topped with crab mixture and croutons.

Local Favorite

Cooter (Turtle) Soup

2 pounds "Cooter" meat- preferably female yellow belly turtle
1 large onion, chopped
1 small Irish potato, diced
Red pepper to taste
Salt to taste
12 whole cloves
2 teaspoons allspice
2 tablespoons Worcestershire
Flour to thicken
6 Cooter eggs
3 tablespoons dry sherry
1 lemon thinly sliced

In a large stockpot over medium-high heat, boil Cooter, onion and potato 2 hours or until meat drops from bones. Remove all bones and skins from meat; cube meat and return to stock. Add red pepper, salt, cloves, allspice and Worcestershire; return to a simmer for 20 minutes. Brown flour in skillet over medium heat; add 1 cup stock. Mix to form smooth paste and stir into soup to thicken. Twenty minutes before serving, add eggs. Add sherry and garnish with thin slices of lemon.

Local Favorite

The Whistle Stop at the American Café

109 South Main Street
Travelers Rest, SC 29690
864-WHISTLE (944-7853)
www.whistlestopattheamericancafe.com
Find us on Facebook

Vickie Vernon Hawkins is the third-generation owner of the Whistle Stop Café—Upstate's oldest restaurant. Her grandfather, Troy Styles, Sr., purchased the American Café in 1945. Later operated by her uncle, Troy Styles, Jr., from the mid-1960's until his retirement, the Café was purchased by Vickie in 2014. She completely renovated it, tripling its size with added outdoor rooftop dining and a little red caboose, which caters to the Swamp Rabbit Trail. Specializing in "Soulicious" Southern cuisine, the WSC is renowned for its shrimp 'n' grits, fried green tomatoes, and more. If you love trains, history, and great food, visit the Whistle Stop, where the past is always present.

Monday – Thursday: 11:00 am to 8:30 pm
Friday – Saturday: 11:00 am to 9:30 pm
Sunday: 11:00 am to 3:00 pm

Miss Vickie's
Southern Pecan Pie

This recipe has been handed down from my grandmother, Lillian Style, to my mother, Dolores Vernon, and now to me.

10 tablespoons butter
2 cups light brown sugar
2 pinches salt
2 cups white Karo syrup
6 large eggs, well beaten
2 teaspoons vanilla extract
2 pie shells
2 cups crushed pecans, divided

Preheat oven to 350°. In a saucepan over medium heat, melt butter, stirring frequently until lightly browned. (This is the secret to a delicious pecan pie!) Add sugar, salt and syrup to butter; with a hand mixer on medium speed, blend until well combined. Add eggs and vanilla; continue blending until all sugar is completely dissolved. Pour into pie shells. Add 1 cup pecans to each pie, pressing pecans under liquid mixture so they will caramelize. Bake 45 minutes and turn oven off. Leave pies in oven an additional 5 to 7 minutes until centers slightly jiggle when moved. Remove and let cool 3 to 4 hours before cutting. Makes 2 pies.

Restaurant Recipe

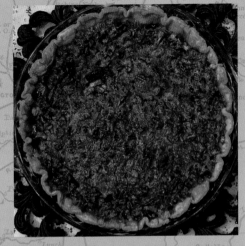

The Steak House Cafeteria

316 East Main Street
Walhalla, SC 29621
864-638-3311
www.thesteakhousecafeteria.com
Find us on Facebook

Gloria and Abed Yassen opened The Steak House Cafeteria in April 1973. Gloria, then an employee at Oconee Social Services, rode by Seigler's Steak House to discover it had closed for business. After some deliberation, she and Abed decided to purchase the business and building. T-bone steaks and grits were menu staples in those early days, but short orders, like fried flounder and hamburger steak, were soon added. The restaurant is now in its fifth decade of business, a dream made possible by family, friends, and guests who have supported it through the years. The Steak House Cafeteria family cherishes its past and looks forward to a wonderful future.

Thursday – Saturday: 11:00 am to 8:00 pm
Sunday: 10:45 am to 3:00 pm

Shrimp Athena

1 pound large shrimp,
 peeled and deveined

2 tablespoons flour

1 (8-ounce) package linguini

1 tablespoon olive oil

2 tablespoons butter

4 garlic cloves, minced

¾ cup white wine

⅓ cup heavy cream (or half-and-half)

1 cup pitted kalamata olives, drained

1 pint grape tomatoes

4 cups baby spinach

Salt and pepper to taste

1 cup crumbled feta cheese

Toss shrimp in flour to coat; set aside. In a large pot, boil salted water and cook pasta per package directions; drain well and set aside. In a large skillet over medium-high heat, add oil and butter; add garlic and floured shrimp and sauté 1 minute. Add wine and cream; toss and cook 1 minute. Add olives and tomatoes; cook 2 minutes. Mix in pasta and spinach. Cook until spinach wilts. Remove from heat and season with salt and pepper to taste. Serve topped with feta cheese.

Local Favorite

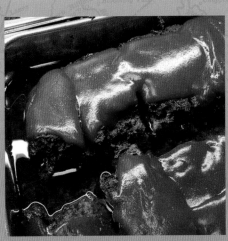

Fresh Peach Iced Tea

3 large fresh peaches, cubed
5 cups water, divided, plus
more to fill pitcher
2 cups sugar plus more to taste
1 lemon, zested
2 to 3 family size tea bags

In a large saucepan, add peaches, 2 cups water, sugar and lemon zest. Cover and bring to light simmer until peaches are soft, 15 to 20 minutes. Using a potato masher, mash peaches to release more juice. Continue to simmer another 10 minutes. Strain peach mixture, discarding solid; set aside. Boil 3 cups water; place tea bags in water and steep for 10 to 15 minutes. Discard tea bags. Add tea to a large pitcher and stir in peach syrup. Gradually add water, stirring well, until pitcher is full. Add more sugar if desired. Refrigerate until cold. Stir before serving and pour over ice. Garnish with mint and fresh peach slices if desired.

Local Favorite

Oyster Fritters

4 eggs, separated
1 tablespoon minced onion, optional
½ teaspoon salt
⅛ teaspoon pepper
6 tablespoons flour
1 cup drained and chopped oysters

Beat egg yolks until thick and creamy. Add onion, salt and pepper. Stir in flour, a little at a time, until all is incorporated. Beat egg whites until stiff. Fold in oysters and egg whites. Drop by spoonfuls in hot grease. Serves 5.

Local Favorite

Shortcake for Strawberry Shortcake

2 cups all-purpose flour
4 teaspoons baking powder
1 teaspoon salt
4 tablespoons shortening
1 egg, beaten until light
1 cup milk
1 tablespoon sugar

Preheat oven to 400°. Sift together flour, baking powder and salt. Add shortening and egg; mix well. Add milk and sugar; mix well. Pour batter into a 9x9-inch baking dish. Bake 20 minutes. Remove and cool. Pour fresh strawberries on top.

Local Favorite

Sliced Candied Potatoes

**4 large sweet potatoes,
thinly sliced**

1 cup light brown sugar

1 cup white sugar

2½ tablespoons flour

Dash salt

4 tablespoons butter, melted

1 teaspoon lemon flavoring

Preheat oven to 350°. Place potatoes in a buttered 9x13-inch baking dish. Mix sugars with four and salt; sprinkle over potatoes. Combine butter with lemon flavoring and drizzle over top. Add ½ cup hot water to allow potatoes to cook. Bake 30 minutes or until potatoes are tender and candied.

Local Favorite

Hot Pizza Dip

**1 (8-ounce) package cream
cheese, softened**

½ teaspoon dried oregano

½ teaspoon dried parsley

¼ teaspoon dried basil

**1 cup shredded mozzarella
cheese, divided**

1 cup grated Parmesan cheese, divided

1 cup pizza sauce

2 tablespoons chopped green bell pepper

2 ounces pepperoni sausage, chopped

2 tablespoons sliced black olives

In a small bowl, mix together cream cheese, oregano, parsley and basil. Spread mixture in the bottom of a 9-inch pie plate, or a shallow microwave-safe dish. Sprinkle half the mozzarella cheese and half the Parmesan cheese on top of the cream cheese mixture. Spread pizza sauce over all. Sprinkle with remaining cheeses, then top with green pepper, pepperoni and olive slices. Cover, and microwave for 5 minutes. Serve hot.

Local Favorite

Midlands

The VILLAGE Café

EAT • DRINK • GELATO

110 Coach Light Way
Aiken, SC 29803
803-640-0247
www.thevillagecafeaiken.com • Find us on
Facebook, Instagram, TripAdvisor & Yelp

The Village Café was created with customers in mind. This upscale counter-service café strives to provide guests with delicious, quality food, drink, and gelato, a creamier Italian ice cream with more flavor and less fat than American ice cream. Serving breakfast, lunch, and early evening dessert, The Village Café is here to meet your needs any time of day. Sip on one of the rich coffee flavors or have a cup of tea to start your day off right. You may also unwind with a beer or a glass of fine wine while you enjoy a house-made sandwich or soup. The Village Café team looks forward to your visit.

Monday – Wednesday:
7:30 am to 4:00 pm
Thursday – Saturday:
7:30 am to 8:00 pm

Village Chicken Salad

4 pounds organic chicken breast,
trimmed and lightly pounded

Vegetable stock
(enough to cover chicken)

2 tablespoons minced red onion

1 cup diced celery

¼ cup honey

4 tablespoons Dijon mustard

4 tablespoons whole-grain mustard

1 cup Greek yogurt

1 cup mayonnaise

½ cup dried cranberries

½ cup chopped walnuts

2 teaspoons dried tarragon

¼ teaspoon each salt and pepper

Add chicken to a large stockpot and cover with vegetable stock; heat until barely simmering. Poach 20 minutes, then carefully remove from pot and shock in a large pot of ice water. Drain, shred chicken and add to a large mixing bowl. Add remaining ingredients and mix until well combined; chill. Adjust seasoning as needed.

Restaurant Recipe

Village Creamy Citrus Mustard Dressing

1 cup sour cream

½ cup yogurt

2 cups mayonnaise

1 tablespoon minced shallots

1 lime, juiced and zested

1 lemon, zested

¼ cup lemon juice

4 tablespoons Dijon mustard

½ teaspoon chopped garlic

½ teaspoon each salt and pepper

In a bowl, mix all ingredients together until well combined.

Restaurant Recipe

House Baked Pastrami every Friday

Country Captain Chicken

3 tablespoons butter, divided
1½ cups rice
⅔ cup flour
1 rounded tablespoon sweet paprika
4 (6-ounce) boneless
skinless chicken breasts
3 boneless, skinless chicken thighs
Salt and pepper
2 tablespoons extra virgin olive oil
1 green bell pepper, chopped
1 red bell pepper, chopped
1 medium onion, chopped
2 to 3 garlic cloves, smashed
1 tablespoon curry powder
1 cup chicken stock
1 (14.5-ounce) can diced tomatoes
¼ cup golden raisins
1 (2-ounce) package sliced almonds
3 scallions, chopped, for garnish

In a medium saucepan bring 2. cups water to a boil. Add 1 tablespoon butter and rice; return to a boil. Reduce heat to low, cover and cook 20 minutes or until rice is tender. Turn off heat; fluff rice with a fork. Combine flour and paprika in a shallow dish. Cut each breast and thigh in half on an angle and season with salt and pepper. Coat chicken in seasoned flour. Heat large skillet over medium heat; add oil. Brown chicken 3 minutes on each side; remove and set aside. Add remaining butter to pan; stir in bell peppers, onion and garlic. Season with salt and pepper and sauté 5 to 7 minutes. Add curry powder, stock, tomatoes and raisins. Slide chicken back into pan and simmer over moderate heat 5 minutes to combine flavors and finish cooking chicken. Garnish chicken with sliced almonds and rice with chopped scallions.

Local Favorite

Slow Cooker BBQ

1 (5-pound) bone-in pork shoulder roast
1 tablespoon salt
Ground black pepper
1½ cups apple cider vinegar
2 tablespoons brown sugar
1½ tablespoons hot pepper sauce
2 teaspoons cayenne pepper
2 teaspoons crushed red pepper flakes

Place pork in slow cooker and season with salt and pepper. Pour vinegar around pork. Cover and cook on low for 12 hours, until pork easily pulls apart. Remove pork from slow cooker and discard any bones. Strain liquid and save 2 cups; discard any extra. Shred pork using tongs or two forks and return to slow cooker. Stir brown sugar, hot pepper sauce, cayenne pepper and red pepper flakes into reserved stock. Stir into pork in slow cooker. Cover and keep on low until serving.

Local Favorite

Baked Potato Sauce

A great alternative to sour cream.

1 cup mayonnaise
½ cup grated Parmesan cheese
¼ cup grated onion
¼ cup butter, softened
½ teaspoon hot pepper sauce

Combine all ingredients. This mixture will keep indefinitely under refrigeration.

Local Favorite

WHISKEY ALLEY

227 The Alley
Aiken, SC 29801
803-226-0579
www.whiskeyalley.com • Find us on Facebook

On the surface, Whiskey Alley is a whiskey bar, but as you peel back the layers, you find something so much more. The bartender, Chunky, provides a wide selection of great whiskeys as well as craft cocktails, beer, and wines. The true treasure of this place is the handcrafted cuisine by Chef Chad Jajczyk. Stop in for the best burger or fish and chips in town, or try one of the amazing selections from the constantly changing specials menu. The Whiskey Alley team takes their craft very seriously, but they never take themselves too seriously. Come in, have fun, and enjoy yourself.

Tuesday – Saturday: 4:00 pm until

Whiskey Alley Jerky

1 Spanish onion, diced

4 tablespoons chopped fresh garlic

2 teaspoons cracked black pepper
or to taste

1½ cups light brown sugar

3 cups soy sauce

¼ cup sesame oil

½ cup Sriracha sauce

1 cup Worcestershire sauce

1 cup balsamic vinegar

2 cups pineapple juice

3 tablespoons toasted sesame seeds

4 teaspoons red pepper flakes

3 pounds flank steak, sliced
into ⅛-inch strips

In a zip-close plastic bag, combine all ingredients except steak; gently shake to combine. Add steak and seal bag. Massage gently to incorporate marinade throughout steak. Carefully press air out of bag, reseal and refrigerate overnight. Set out dehydrator racks and arrange steak slices in a single layer. Return racks to dehydrator. Set dehydrator to 150° and dry 4 to 5 hours or until jerky is chewy but not yet tacky.

Restaurant Recipe

Whiskey Alley Pimento Cheese

1 pound sharp Cheddar cheese, grated

4 ounces cream cheese

⅛ cup small-diced roasted red peppers

½ cup Duke's mayonnaise

4 tablespoons sour cream

1 tablespoon Dijon mustard

1 tablespoon Valentina hot sauce

½ teaspoon coarse black pepper

1 teaspoon onion powder

1 teaspoon garlic powder

½ cup lager beer

Salt and pepper to taste

Mix all ingredients, except salt and pepper, in the bowl of a stand mixer. Season with salt and pepper; mix once more. Store in refrigerator for up to 1 week in a tightly sealed bowl.

Restaurant Recipe

WHERE CAN YOU FIND HEALING FOR THE BODY, MIND AND SPIRIT?

God's Acre Healing Springs is known for its rich history and healing powers. Today, many South Carolinians still hold the site sacred, traveling hours to collect water from the springs. A nearby historical marker reads, "The waters, by analysis, are exceptionally pure and contain healthful minerals. People today, as in the past, believe they truly are Healing Springs."

The springs' mineral waters flow from nearby artesian wells and have been a source of local folklore for many, many years. Native Americans who lived near the site believed the waters were sacred because of the healing properties.

According to legend, four British soldiers were severely wounded during the American Revolution in a battle at nearby Windy Hill Creek. They, along with two men left behind to bury them when they died, were rescued by Native Americans. Six months after being brought to the springs, every soldier was restored to fighting health merely by drinking and bathing in the springs. They returned to their post in Charleston, crediting the springs' waters with their miraculous recovery.

GOD'S ACRE HEALING SPRINGS

ACCORDING TO TRADITION, THE INDIANS REVERENCED THE WATER FOR ITS HEALING PROPERTIES AS A GIFT FROM THE GREAT SPIRIT.

THEY LED THE BRITISH WOUNDED TO THEIR SECRET WATERS DURING THE AMERICAN REVOLUTION AND THE WOUNDED WERE HEALED.

THIS HISTORICAL PROPERTY HAS BEEN DEEDED TO GOD FOR PUBLIC USE. PLEASE REVERE GOD BY KEEPING IT CLEAN.

Why is it called God's Acre? After Native Americans sold the springs to a trader named Nathaniel Walker for corn, the land passed through many hands before it was eventually purchased by Lute Boylston. A monument notes that the acre of land surrounding the springs was "Deeded to Almighty God" by Mr. Boylston in 1944.

The springs are located behind Healing Springs Baptist Church, and Healing Springs Country Store is just around the corner. What is better when traveling the back roads than stopping for some cold refreshment? Stopping in a beautiful area for a cool drink of beverage that is tasty... and free... and may heal your body, mind, and soul.

God's Acre Healing Springs

**Highway 3 and
Healing Springs Road
Blackville, SC 29817**

GOD'S ACRE HEALING SPRINGS

By tradition, Healing Springs got its name during the Revolutionary War. In 1781 after a bloody battle at nearby Windy Hill Creek, four wounded Tories sent inland from Charleston by General Banastre (The Butcher) Tarleton were left in the care of two comrades who had orders to bury them when they died. Luckily, Native Americans found them and took them to their secret, sacred, healing springs. Six months later the Charleston Garrison was astonished by the reappearance of the six men. All were strong and healthy.

(Continued on other side)

Miller's Bread Basket

483 Main Street
Blackville, SC 29817
803-284-3117
www.millersbreadbasket.com • Find us on Facebook

Miller's Bread Basket opened in 1987 as a family-owned restaurant serving home-cooked, Amish-Mennonite-style foods. Over the years, as the children married, had children and some moved away, the restaurant continued operation under its founders. Mervin and Anna Miller purchased the business from the original owners in late 2014 and began operating the restaurant in January 2015, keeping the same employees and preserving the theme of good, home-cooked meals and fresh, homemade breads and desserts. Many new things are in store for the restaurant and the Miller's team hopes you will stick around to see them unfold.

Tuesday & Wednesday: 11:00 am to 2:00 pm
Thursday & Friday: 11:00 to 8:00 pm
Saturday: 7:00 am to 2:00 pm

Close to Healing Springs

Chicken Dressing

6 eggs, lightly beaten

5 cups milk

1 (49.25-ounce) can cream of celery soup

½ heaping cup mayonnaise

4½ cups chicken stock

2½ loaves homemade white bread,
toasted and torn into pieces

½ loaf garlic-onion bread,
torn into pieces

8 cups chopped dark meat chicken

3 cups chopped onions

8 cups shredded sharp Cheddar cheese

1½ teaspoons celery salt

Preheat oven to 325°. In a large bowl, add eggs, milk, soup, mayonnaise and stock; mix well. Add remaining ingredients, mixing until bread and chicken are well incorporated. Pour into 2 treated 9x13-inch pans. Bake, uncovered, 1 hour or until set and top is just starting to brown.

Restaurant Recipe

Shoo-Fly Pie

¾ cup white sugar

1 cup brown sugar

7 cups molasses

8 eggs

2 teaspoons baking soda

6 cups hot water

7 (10-inch) pie shells

Crumb Mixture:

10¾ cups flour

4½ cups bread flour

6 cups brown sugar

2 cups lard

1 tablespoon baking soda

1 tablespoon cream of tartar

Preheat oven to 325°. In a large bowl, combine sugars and molasses; beat in eggs. In another bowl, mix baking soda into hot water; whisk into sugar mixture and set aside. In a stand mixer with a paddle attachment, combine ingredients for Crumb Mixture; mix until well combined. Add 6 cups Crumb Mixture to sugar mixture; whisk until smooth. Distribute filling evenly among pie shells. Top pies evenly with remaining Crumb Mixture, covering filling entirely. Bake 45 minutes, or until set.

Restaurant Recipe

Eatery at the Depot

7501 Freedom Road
Branchville, SC 29432
803-274-8001
Find us on Facebook

Eatery at the Depot is located in the historic railroad depot in Branchville. It is the oldest railroad junction in the world. Three Presidents of the United States have dined at the restaurant. Menu highlights are fresh fried seafood, marinated and grilled chicken breast and pork tenderloin, seasonal sides, and homemade desserts. Thursday's special is shrimp and grits, and Friday and Saturday's special is prime rib. Catering and private parties are also available. Follow Eatery at the Depot on Facebook to keep up with the latest in railside dining.

Thursday, Saturday & Sunday: 6:00 pm to 8:30 pm
Friday: 6:00 pm to 9:00 pm

Crab Dip

12 ounces cream cheese, softened
6 cups Hellman's Mayonnaise
3 dashes hot sauce
1 tablespoon Worcestershire sauce
1 teaspoon minced garlic
Cracked pepper to taste
1 pound lump crabmeat
3 cups shredded mild Cheddar cheese
Captain's Wafer crackers for dipping

In a bowl, combine first 6 ingredients and mix well. Gently fold in crabmeat and cheese until well combined. Chill 2 hours. Serve with Captain's Wafer crackers. Serves a crowd.

Restaurant Recipe

Waffles

2 cups flour
1 heaping teaspoon baking powder
Pinch salt
2 eggs, beaten
1¼ cups milk
1 tablespoon butter, melted

Combine all ingredients. Set aside while waffle iron heats. Pour batter in waffle iron and cook until browned to your taste.

Local Favorite

Stuffed Baked Apples

4 baking apples
⅓ cup dried cranberries
⅓ cup slivered almonds
½ teaspoon cinnamon
½ teaspoon nutmeg
2 tablespoons honey
½ cup orange juice concentrate

Preheat oven to 325°. Wash apples and core about three quarters of the way down, leaving a little in bottom. In a bowl, combine cranberries, almonds, cinnamon and nutmeg; mix well. Stuff each apple with cranberry mixture. Place in a 9-inch square baking dish. In same bowl, combine honey and orange juice with 2 cups water; mix well. Pour over apples. Bake 30 to 40 minutes, or until apples are tender.

Local Favorite

Apple Crisp

6 Granny Smith apples, peeled,
cored and sliced
1½ cups sugar, divided
1½ cups self-rising flour
1½ teaspoons cinnamon
1 teaspoon nutmeg
¾ cup butter

Preheat oven to 375°. Grease and flour a 9x13-inch glass dish; set aside. Place apple slices in a bowl and toss with 1/2 cup sugar. Layer in casserole dish. In same bowl, combine flour, cinnamon and nutmeg with remaining sugar; mix well. Evenly distribute over apples. Dot with butter. Bake 30 minutes.

Local Favorite

Chicken Pot Pie

4 cups chopped cooked chicken

2 (10.75-ounce) cans cream of chicken soup

1 cup chicken broth

1 teaspoon chicken base

1 (16-ounce) bag frozen mixed vegetables

Salt and pepper to taste

2 hard-boiled eggs, diced

1 stick butter, melted

1 cup milk

1 cup self-rising flour

1 teaspoon baking powder

Preheat oven to 350°. In a large bowl, mix together chicken, soup, broth, chicken base, vegetables, salt, pepper and eggs. Pour into a buttered 2-quart casserole. Mix butter, milk, flour and baking powder. Pour over chicken mixture. Bake 45 minutes to 1 hour or until crust is golden brown.

Local Favorite

Strawberry Butter

4 sticks butter, softened

½ cup powdered sugar

1 cup finely diced, sweet strawberries

Using a hand mixer, cream butter in a large bowl until whipped and smooth. Mix in sugar, beating 1 minute. Fold in strawberries until butter is light pink and creamy. Pour onto parchment paper or wax paper and form into a roll, twisting ends of paper to seal. Refrigerate until ready to use. Great on hot pancakes, waffles or biscuits. When strawberries are in season, make several and freeze for a fresh taste of spring any time of the year.

Local Favorite

Main Street Retreat Bar & Grill

1007 Old North Main Street
Clover, SC 29710
803-222-4467
www.mainstretreat.com • Find us on Facebook

Don't let the location fool you. Main Street Retreat is a quaint little bar and grill, which offers some of the best food in Clover. Featuring delicious hand-breaded onion rings, award-winning burgers, hand-cut steaks, various sandwiches, and so much more, there is something for everyone to enjoy. Relax in the charm of the rustic, indoor atmosphere, or dine outside on the covered porch or around the fire pit on the paver patio. All menu items are made to order, so relax with your favorite beverage while the chef prepares your meal. The Main Street Retreat team looks forward to serving you and making you part of the family.

Tuesday – Thursday: 11:00 am to 10:00 pm
Friday & Saturday: 11:00 am to 11:00 pm
Sunday: 11:00 am to 9:00 pm

Deep-Fried Brownies

1 box chocolate fudge brownie mix
plus ingredients to prepare
3 tablespoons sugar
9 tablespoons powdered sugar
2 eggs
2½ cups all-purpose flour
Ice cream, whipped cream, chocolate
syrup and maraschino cherries, optional

Prepare brownies according to package directions; cool before cutting. Separate brownies and place on a baking sheet lined with parchment paper; chill in freezer. Meanwhile, preheat deep fryer to 350°. In a bowl, whisk together sugar, powdered sugar and eggs until smooth; whisk in 1½ cups water. Whisk in flour until thickened. Remove brownies from freezer. Coat brownie evenly in batter, and, using tongs, hold in deep fryer 10 seconds to firm up coating. Let go of brownie and fry, turning accordingly, until golden brown. Drain on paper towels and repeat with remaining brownies. Plate brownies and top with ice cream, whipped cream, chocolate syrup or cherries, if desired.

Restaurant Recipe

Blackened Prime Rib

Blackening Rub:

½ cup each kosher salt, paprika,
granulated garlic and black pepper
¼ cup each cayenne pepper, onion
powder, dried oregano and dried thyme

In a large bowl, mix all ingredients until well combined.

1 (5-pound) prime rib-eye loin
1 beef bouillon cube

Preheat oven to 400°, leaving oven door closed 1 hour after temperature is reached. Generously apply Blackening Rub over ribeye, reserving ¼ cup; cover ribeye and set aside. After 1 hour, uncover ribeye and place in oven; cook 45 minutes. Leaving door shut, turn off oven and allow ribeye to rest in oven 30 to 45 minutes more. Remove ribeye and rest on counter 10 to 15 minutes. Meanwhile make au jus; bring 2 cups water with bouillon cube to boil. Add reserved Blackening Rub and simmer while prime rib cools. Slice prime rib and serve with au jus.

Restaurant Recipe

Crave Artisan Specialty Market & Café

2843 Millwood Avenue
Columbia, SC 29205
803-254-1001
www.cravespecialties.com • Find us on Facebook

In March 2016, John Brunty and partners opened Crave Artisan Specialty Market & Café to sell regional products, like jams, honey, grits, and so much more. Later that year, the group added a kitchen to showcase how well all of the flavors blended and enjoyed immediate success. By April 2017, it was clear that Crave needed professional help, which arrived in the form of Ola Helsing, a chef trained at the French Culinary Institute in New York City. Soon shelves began disappearing to make room for tables, and the accolades began pouring in. Stop by Crave Artisan Specialty Market & Café for regional products, artisanal sandwiches, tomato pies, chicken pot pies, quiches, salads, and more.

Market:
Monday – Saturday: 9:00 am to 6:00 pm
Café:
Monday – Saturday: 10:30 am to 4:00 pm

Creamy Berry Custard Bars

Crust:

1½ cups all-purpose flour
½ cup sugar
½ teaspoon salt
2 sticks butter, cut into small pieces

Preheat oven to 350°. Mix flour, sugar and salt in a bowl; cut in butter until crumbly. Press mixture into a lightly greased 9x13-inch baking dish. Bake about 15 minutes or until golden brown. Remove from oven to cool.

Filling:

⅓ cup all-purpose flour
1½ cups sugar
1½ cups heavy cream
3 eggs, lightly beaten
5 cups mixed sliced strawberries and whole blueberries
½ teaspoon vanilla extract

Mix flour and sugar in a large bowl. Stir in cream and eggs. Stir in berries and vanilla. Pour over baked crust. Bake at 350° for 40 minutes or until set. Remove from oven; cool to room temperature.

Topping:

2 (3-ounce) packages cream cheese, softened
½ cup sugar
½ teaspoon vanilla extract
1 cup whipped cream

In a bowl, beat cream cheese and sugar until smooth. Beat in vanilla. Fold in whipped cream. Spread over custard. Cover and refrigerate several hours; cut into bars and enjoy.

Restaurant Recipe

Tomato Cucumber Salad

5 medium cucumbers
7 medium tomatoes
½ large red onion
3 tablespoons granulated garlic
1 cup red wine vinegar
1 cup canola oil
3 tablespoons dried dill
2 tablespoons dried parsley
1 tablespoons each salt and pepper
Freshly ground pepper

Peel cucumbers, cut in half lengthwise and scoop out seeds with a spoon; cut into thin slices and add to a large bowl. Give tomatoes a medium dice and onion a small dice; add to bowl with cucumber. Gently fold in remaining ingredients. Taste and adjust seasoning if necessary.

Restaurant Recipe

WHERE CAN YOU FIND THE WORLD'S LARGEST KID?

Edventure Children's Museum in Columbia is home to Eddie—a 40-foot-tall, 17-ton, 10-year-old boy. As if that's not amazing enough, Eddie is a completely hands-on exhibit, allowing visitors to the museum to climb through his heart, brain, and stomach. You can even slide out of his intestines.

If you tire of quiet museums where you are constantly reminding your children "don't touch," Edventure is the place to be. There are 300 exhibits spread over 92,000 square feet of interactive, hands-on fun for kids 12 and younger.

Just a few of the exhibits to explore include Busy Bee Farm, Body Detectives, The Neighborhood Market, a Cooking Lab, AutoWorks, Critter Garden, and Dalmation Station. In spring and summer, children will enjoy the outdoor exhibit called "Blooming Butterflies," where they can personally interact with these fascinating insects.

Drop by to say hi to Eddie, and stay for the rest of the fun.

Edventure

**211 Gervais Street
Columbia, SC 29201
803-779-3100
www.edventure.org**

Di Prato's Delicatessen

342 Pickens Street
Columbia, SC 29205
803-779-0606
www.dipratos.com • Find us on Facebook

Di Prato's Delicatessen opened May 2004, affording patrons a rewarding escape from ordinary fare. Featuring delectable food, beautiful décor, and friendly service, this charming restaurant is located in the heart of Columbia between the University of South Carolina and 5 Points. Driving up, you'll notice the rich, red brick set off by greenery and spacious windows where light pours in. You could say a Southern breeze laden with Italian accents drifts through this New York-style delicatessen. Dine on the patio where the glassy splash of falling water melts away concerns. The pita chips and pimento cheese are a real treat. Stop by today for the full Di Prato's experience.

Lunch:
Daily: 10:00 am to 4:00 pm
Brunch:
Saturday & Sunday: 10:00 am to 2:00 pm

Tomato-Basil Bisque with Goat Cheese

3 tablespoons olive oil

2 red onions, chopped

Salt and black pepper

3 garlic cloves, minced

1 (28-ounce) can crushed tomatoes

4 cups chicken stock

1 cup heavy cream

1 bunch basil, torn into small bite-size pieces

Goat cheese for garnish

Heat olive oil in medium stockpot over medium heat. Add onions and season with salt and pepper to taste; cook until onions are tender and golden brown, about 5 to 8 minutes. Add garlic and cook 1 minute. Stir in tomatoes and chicken stock; season with additional salt and pepper. Bring mixture to a boil, then lower heat. Simmer at least 15 to 20 minutes. Purée mixture with an immersion blender. Stir in cream and basil and simmer at least 20 to 30 minutes to thicken. Serve immediately topped with goat cheese.

Restaurant Recipe

Tomato, Cucumber & Red Onion Salad with Fresh Mint

2 large cucumbers, halved lengthwise and seeded

⅓ cup red wine vinegar

1 tablespoon sugar

1 teaspoon salt plus more for seasoning

3 large tomatoes, seeded and coarsely chopped

⅔ cup diced red onion

½ cup chopped fresh mint

3 tablespoon olive oil

Black pepper to taste

Cut cucumber halves into ½-inch pieces. Place in a large bowl with vinegar, sugar and 1 teaspoon salt; let stand at room temperature about 1 hour, stirring occasionally. Add tomatoes, red onions, mint and olive oil; mix carefully. Season with salt and pepper.

Restaurant Recipe

STICKY ★ WINGS

2Mothers

SOUTHERN COOKING

5 Lake Caroline Way
Columbia, SC 29229
803-764-1793
Find us on Facebook

Come on out to 2Mothers Southern Cooking. Opened in 2014, this family-owned-and-operated restaurant serves up delicious Southern food just like your mom used to make. Guests will enjoy dishes like Momma Mary's Fried Chicken, veggie plates, sticky wings, fried flounder, fried pork chops, and more. You don't want to miss out on dessert, so make sure you try the peach cobbler, banana pudding, or red velvet cake. 2Mothers also has a Granny's Kids Meal menu for guests with little ones, so there truly is something on the menu to please everyone in your family. Stop by 2Mothers Southern Cooking today and discover "your home away from home."

Tuesday – Saturday: 11:30 am to 7:30 pm

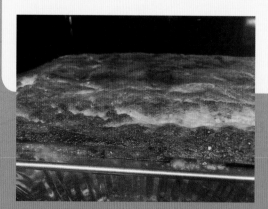

Smothered Pork Chops

4 to 6 pork chops
2 teaspoons hot sauce
¼ teaspoon sea salt
¼ teaspoon black pepper
1¼ cups flour, divided
2 tablespoons onion powder
½ teaspoon garlic powder
1 teaspoon paprika
½ cup vegetable oil
1 large onion, diced
2 cups chicken stock
¼ cup buttermilk

Season dry pork chops with hot sauce, salt and pepper. In a bowl, combine 1 cup flour, onion powder, garlic powder and paprika. Dredge chops in flour mixture on both sides until fully coated. Heat a large frying pan over medium heat; add vegetable oil. Once hot, fry chops in oil, 5 to 6 minutes each side; drain on paper towels. Add onion to pan and sauté 4 to 5 minutes. Add remaining flour and whisk until mixture resembles a paste. Slowly whisk in stock; increase heat and allow mixture to thicken, stirring occasionally. Once thickened, stir in buttermilk. Place chops in pan and simmer over medium-low heat 25 to 30 minutes or until chops are tender.

Restaurant Recipe

Sweatman's Bar-B-Que

1427 Eutaw Road
Holly Hill, SC 29059
803-496-1227
www.sweatmansbbq.com • Find us on Facebook

Bub and Margie Sweatman first opened a small barbecue place in 1959 but later closed it, from then on cooking only for family and friends. Still, their desire to open a barbecue restaurant remained, and, after purchasing an old farmhouse, Sweatman's Bar-B-Que officially opened for business in 1977. Every week, whole hogs are cooked over hot coals, smoked to perfect tenderness and flavor using oak, hickory, and pecan woods. The secret is in basting with Sweatman's special mustard-based sauce. Come on out to Sweatman's Bar-B-Que and sample the long, rich tradition of delicious barbecue.

Friday & Saturday: 11:30 am to 8:00 pm

Bourbon Balls

2½ cups crushed vanilla wafers
1 cup pecans
2 tablespoons cocoa powder
1 cup powdered sugar
3 tablespoons light Karo syrup
¼ cup bourbon

Grind vanilla wafers and pecans in a food processor. In a bowl, mix cocoa and sugar together; stir in wafer-pecan mixture. In another bowl, stir Karo into bourbon and pour over dry ingredients; mix until moist. Shape into small balls and roll in powdered sugar. Store in a sealable container.

Local Favorite

Rice-Stuffed Tomatoes

8 medium-sized ripe tomatoes
Salt
1 tablespoon extra-virgin olive oil
1 medium onion, diced
1 small garlic clove, minced
6 slices bacon, chopped
2 tablespoons minced sweet basil
1 tablespoon minced parsley
½ cup halfway cooked and drained rice
½ cup grated Fontina
(or Romano) cheese

Preheat oven to 375°. Cut off tops of tomatoes; reserve. Using a spoon, scoop pulp into a fine mesh strainer placed over a bowl. Sprinkle salt around inside of each tomato. Mash pulp through strainer into bowl and discard seeds; set aside. In a skillet over medium heat, sauté onion, garlic and bacon in olive oil until onion is transparent and bacon is crisp. Add tomato pulp, basil and parsley to pan and mix well. Cook 2 to 3 minutes; remove from heat. Add rice and mix thoroughly. Add cheese and mix well. If needed, adjust salt to taste. Line a baking dish with parchment paper and arrange tomatoes cut side up. Stuff each with a generous 1 to 2 spoonsful of rice mixture until slightly overflowing. Replace tomato tops and cover dish with foil. Bake 30 minutes on center rack of oven. Uncover and bake another 15 minutes. Remove from oven and cool 5 minutes before serving.

Local Favorite

Easy Baked Beans

1 cup chopped bacon
1 small onion, chopped
2 tablespoons cider vinegar
1 (16-ounce) can baked beans
1 (15-ounce) can pork and beans
⅓ cup barbecue sauce

In a 2-quart saucepan over medium heat, cook bacon until it begins to brown. Add onion and vinegar; cook 3 to 5 minutes or until onion is tender. Stir in remaining ingredients; bring to a boil. Reduce heat to medium low; cook uncovered 5 minutes, stirring occasionally. Serve.

Local Favorite

Garlic Cheese

Do not use pre-shredded cheese for this recipe. It contains a preservative and does not keep well.

4 (8-ounce) packages cream cheese, softened

4 to 6 garlic cloves, finely grated

1 cup mayonnaise

1 (2-pound) block extra sharp Cheddar cheese, grated

Leave a stand mixer on during the entire prep process. Add cream cheese to mixing bowl and beat until smooth. Add 1 to 2 tablespoons garlic and 2 tablespoons mayonnaise. Remember: continue to beat through the whole process, about 5 minutes between each addition. Add a third of the cheese. Continue to add garlic and mayonnaise, 1 to 2 tablespoons at a time, and cheese in thirds until all is incorporated. Turn off mixer and cover with a damp kitchen towel; set aside 1 hour. May be stored in sealed containers and will keep several weeks if properly sealed. The secret is in the beating. The more you beat, the better it gets. This is a great spread on Ritz crackers or as a filling for celery stalks.

Local Favorite

Peanut Butter Fudge

2 cups sugar

⅔ cup milk

4 tablespoons peanut butter

Pinch salt

1 teaspoon vanilla

⅓ cup chopped raisins

In a saucepan over medium-high heat, boil sugar and milk to a soft-ball stage (234° to 240° on a candy thermometer). Remove from heat and add peanut butter, salt and vanilla. Beat until creamy. Add raisins and mix well. Pour into a buttered dish. Cool and cut into squares.

Local Favorite

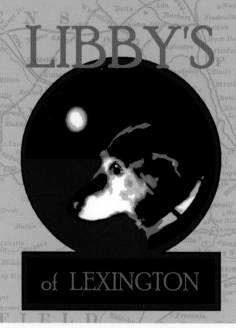

LIBBY'S
of LEXINGTON

Libby's of Lexington

116 West Main Street
Lexington, SC 29072
803-520-4689
www.libbysoflexington.com • Find us on Facebook

Opened in 2010, Libby's of Lexington is a quaint establishment offering a wide variety of food choices in a family-friendly atmosphere. Owner Clint LaCoe brings almost thirty years of experience to the town he grew up in and has called home since 1985. The menu has expanded from Philly cheesesteaks and pizza at his customers' requests to include everything from appetizers, like Shanghai shrimp and bruschetta, to delicious entrées, like fish and chips, fresh-ground burgers, and pizzas, as well as daily specials featuring fresh, locally sourced seafood, house-made pasta dishes, and authentic country cooking. Mr. LaCoe hopes visitors will enjoy Libby's of Lexington as much as he does.

Monday – Saturday: 11:00 am to 10:00 pm

Fish & Chips

Beer–Battered Fish:

1 (12-ounce) can brown ale or dark lager
2 cups high-gluten flour
¼ teaspoon onion powder
¼ teaspoon garlic powder
¼ teaspoon kosher salt
¼ teaspoon lemon pepper
¼ teaspoon chopped fresh dill
¼ teaspoon cayenne pepper
3 pounds cod, cut into 4-ounce strips

Preheat deep fryer to 350°. In a large bowl, make beer batter by mixing together all ingredients except cod. Dip cod strips in batter and drop in fryer 4 to 5 minutes, or until golden brown.

Fries:

3 large potatoes

Wash potatoes and cut into ¾-inch fries. Fry 3 minutes; remove from fryer and cool. Fry again until golden brown. Serves 4 to 5 people.

Restaurant Recipe

WHAT IS THE ONLY CREATURE ON EARTH THAT EATS COTTON?

If you said the boll weevil... you're wrong! As you will learn at the South Carolina Cotton Museum, the answer is humans. According to the museum, mass-produced foods like ice cream, toothpaste, pretzels, cookies, and potato chips contain cotton.

The South Carolina Cotton Museum is an interesting museum that preserves the legacy of cotton and rural life. Exhibits of farm and manufacturing equipment spanning two centuries allow visitors to experience the cotton culture and way of life from the field to the factory.

Between 1920 and 1922, a boll weevil infestation caused cotton production in South Carolina to drop by 70 percent. In the museum's larger-than-life Boll Weevil Exhibit, you will learn how the boll weevil plague destroyed South Carolina's cotton crop by eating the plant (not the cotton). Also included is a giant, custom-built model of the boll weevil, compared to a tiny life-size specimen that sits at its feet.

Other exhibits will take you through cotton's rich agricultural history, with examples of implements ranging from hand tools and baskets used by early cotton growers and pickers and an early Whitney spike gin to old cotton mill machinery exhibited alongside miniature, fully operational versions. Spinning wheels and early looms stand side-by-side with modern spinning and weaving equipment to illustrate the progress of the textile industry. There is also a full-size sharecropper's shack, exhibiting a kitchen, bedroom, and bathroom (slop jar) in one room, and a mechanical cotton farm mule.

Cotton Facts from the Museum

- US paper currency is not paper at all. It's a blend of 75 percent cotton lint and 25 percent linen. A 480-pound bale of cotton can be made into 313,600 $100 bills.

- Sheer cotton muslin, woven in ancient India, was so fine that 73 yards of it weighed one pound.

- Cotton is a member of the mallow family of plants. The Arabian people called it "qatn," which is where we get the word "cotton."

- Eli Whitney's cotton gin wasn't a new idea. The "Churka," invented in India 3,500 years earlier, was efficient at ginning long staple cotton but ineffective on the short staple variety. Whitney's gin was the first to process short staple cotton.

- Mills in Lancashire, England, exported 7,000,000,000 yards of cotton fabric in 1913—an amazing 221.97 yards per second.

South Carolina Cotton Museum

121 West Cedar Lane
Bishopville, SC 29010
803- 484-4497
www.sccotton.org

Antique Mall Café

1528 Main Street
Little Mountain, SC 29075
803-941-7189
Find us on Facebook

The Antique Mall Café is located on the lower level of the Little Mountain Unlimited Antique Mall in the town of Little Mountain. Opened in October 2012, this quaint eatery serves lunch and coffee to antique pickers in need of refreshment after trawling for treasures across the mall's 25,000-square-foot expanse. After you've finished browsing over 70 dealers and 150 booths, stop by the Café for soups, salads, sandwiches, wraps, burgers, and sides. Complete your meal with one of the Café's delicious homemade desserts. The Café is available for special events and offers a variety of catering options. Visit the Antique Mall Café today.

Daily: 11:00 am to 3:00 pm

Corn Dip

1 (16-ounce) bag frozen
whole-kernel corn, thawed

1 stick butter, cubed

1 (8-ounce) package cream
cheese, softened

Chopped jalapeño peppers to taste

Sweet roasted red peppers to taste

1 (8-ounce) block Monterey Jack cheese

Preheat oven to 350°. In a medium
baking dish, add corn, butter and cream
cheese. Add peppers over top. Bake 15
minutes. Remove from oven and grate
cheese over top. Return to oven and bake
another 15 minutes.

Family Favorite

Tropical Fruit Salad

2 (15-ounce) cans fruit cocktail, drained

1 (15-ounce) can mandarin
oranges, drained

1 (15.25-ounce) can crushed
pineapple, drained

1 cup whipped topping

½ cup shredded coconut

¼ cup plain (or vanilla) yogurt

1 cup mini marshmallows

Maraschino cherries, optional

Chopped nuts, optional

Gently mix fruit cocktail, oranges,
pineapple, whipped topping, coconut,
yogurt and marshmallows in a large
bowl. Add additional yogurt to taste,
if desired. Add maraschino cherries or
chopped nuts, if desired. Refrigerate
several hours before serving.

Restaurant Recipe

Porter Jacks Grill

505 South Mill Street
Manning, SC 29102
803-433-5000
www.porterjacksgrill.com • Find us on Facebook

There is seldom a time of gathering that doesn't involve sharing a meal with loved ones and enjoying fellowship. The team at Porter Jacks Grill invites you to share those special times at their table. Opened in May 2017, Porter Jacks' owners were born and raised in Manning. The caring and attentive staff strive to make each meal and visit special. Guests can enjoy everything from appetizers and soups and salads to juicy burgers and perfectly seared steaks. Everything is made from scratch with love by the Porter Jack family, ensuring a home-like feel with each bite.

"They broke bread together with gladness and thankful hearts." –Acts, 2:46

Wednesday – Friday: 11:00 am to 10:00 pm
Saturday: 11:00 am to 11:00 pm
Happy Hour: 4:00 pm to 7:00 pm

Ham Delights

2 sticks butter, softened

3 tablespoons poppy seed

1 teaspoon Worcestershire sauce

3 tablespoons mustard

1 medium onion, minced

3 (12-count) packages Pepperidge Farm
dinner rolls, split in half but
not pulled apart

1 pound boiled ham, thinly sliced

¾ pound Swiss cheese, thinly sliced

Preheat oven to 400°. In a small bowl, cream together butter, poppy seed, Worcestershire, mustard and onion until smooth. Spread half of mixture on bottoms of rolls; place bottoms in baking dish layering with ham and cheese. Replace tops; spread with remaining butter mixture. Bake 10 minutes: remove from oven. Cut rolls apart and enjoy.

Local Favorite

Steven W's

**1100 Main Street
Newberry, SC 29108
803-276-7700
Find us on Facebook**

Open since 1996, Steven W's is a full-service restaurant featuring the finest foods from around the world. Guests will enjoy seafood from off the Carolina coast, Alaska, and Northeastern waters as well as other parts of the world. The menu also features steaks, veal, pork, chicken, pasta, soups, appetizers, and salads. Need a fix for your sweet tooth? Try the Oreo-crusted key lime pie with raspberry sauce, or sample the Almond Basket with raspberry pastry cream, ice cream, strawberries, and chocolate and caramel sauces. The Bistro's philosophy is to leave no food group untouched. Come by Steven W's today for a flavor experience you won't soon forget.

Tuesday – Saturday: 5:30 pm to 9:00 pm

Key Lime Pie

1 (21-ounce) can sweetened
condensed milk
7 tablespoons key lime juice
3 eggs
1 (8-inch) Oreo pie crust

Preheat oven to 400°. Whisk together condensed milk, lime juice and eggs in a bowl. Pour mixture into pie crust. Bake about 15 minutes or until mixture is firmly set into crust but not browning.

Restaurant Recipe

Grilled Tuna with Ginger-Soy Beurre Blanc

1 tuna fillet
Salt and pepper to taste

Grill tuna with salt and pepper to desired doneness.

Ginger-Soy Beurre Blanc:

1 teaspoon diced shallot
1 teaspoon diced garlic
¼ cup white wine
1 stick butter, cut into tablespoons

In a saucepan over medium-low heat, simmer shallot and garlic in wine. Reduce until wine is nearly gone. Set heat to lowest setting and begin whisking in butter, 1 tablespoon at a time, until all butter is incorporated and sauce is thickened. Plate tuna and serve with Ginger-Soy Beurre Blanc.

Restaurant Recipe

Pecan-Crusted Chicken with Blackberry Sauce

1 cup pecans
¼ cup flour
¼ cup breadcrumbs
½ cup half-and-half
1 chicken breast, skinned and trimmed of fat
2 to 3 tablespoons olive oil
6 ounces red wine vinegar
1 shallot, diced
1 (14-ounce) jar blackberry preserves
1 tablespoon heavy cream

Preheat oven to 450°. In a food processor, process pecans into smaller chunks; quickly process flour and breadcrumbs into pecans just until blended. Transfer pecan crusting to a bowl. Add half-and-half to a small bowl. Coat chicken in half-and-half, then firmly press pecans onto both sides of chicken. Add olive oil to a skillet over medium-high heat. Add chicken to skillet and cook on 1 side until nicely browned. Flip chicken and place pan in oven, cooking until internal temperature reaches 165°. Meanwhile, add vinegar and shallot to a small saucepan over medium heat and reduce by half; whisk in preserves. Bring to boil, stir in heavy cream and remove from heat. Plate chicken, and serve with Blackberry Sauce.

Restaurant Recipe

The Original House of Pizza

591 John C. Calhoun Drive
Orangeburg, SC 29115
803-531-4000
www.originalhop.com • Find us on Facebook

Opened in 1981, the Original House of Pizza has been serving the Orangeburg area for more than thirty-five years. The House of Pizza is your one-stop shop for Orangeburg's best and only Greek-Italian fare. This family-owned restaurant offers a range of mouth-watering dishes, from fresh salads and rich pastas to juicy burgers, stuffed calzones, grilled sandwiches, and, of course, the cheesiest pizza. Every dish is prepared in-house and from scratch using original recipes. Let this mom-and-pop eatery with a passion for pizza provide your family with a delicious meal they won't soon forget. Stop by The Original House of Pizza today.

Monday – Thursday: 11:00 am to 9:30 pm
Friday & Saturday: 11:00 am to 10:30 pm

Manestra

⅓ cup olive oil

1 medium onion, diced

4 cloves garlic, minced

2 tablespoons dried oregano

2 (14-ounce) cans stewed tomatoes

3½ cups chicken stock (or water)

½ cup Chardonnay, optional

1 teaspoon salt

½ teaspoon black pepper

1 pound orzo pasta

2 to 3 cups chopped meat of choice (grilled chicken, steak, beef tenderloin, or shrimp)

1 cup crumbled feta cheese

1½ cups shredded mozzarella cheese

¾ cup grated Parmesan cheese

Preheat oven to 400°. In a saucepan over medium heat, heat oil; add onions, sautéing until translucent, about 3 to 5 minutes. Add garlic and oregano; sauté 2 minutes. Drain tomatoes, reserving juice; dice tomatoes and return to juice. Add tomatoes, stock, Chardonnay, salt and pepper to saucepan; bring to a simmer. Evenly layer orzo over bottom of a 9x13-inch baking dish. When tomato mixture reaches a slight boil, transfer to baking dish with orzo and stir. Bake uncovered 20 to 30 minutes, or until pasta is cooked, stirring every 10 minutes or so. Add meat evenly over top of pasta. Add all cheeses. Bake until cheeses are melted. Serves 8.

Restaurant Recipe

Old McCaskills Farm

Low Altitude Imaging

Old McCaskill's Farm

377 Cantey Lane
Rembert, SC 29128
803-432-9537
www.oldmccaskillfarm.com • Find us on Facebook

Old McCaskill's Farm is owned and operated by Kathy and Lee McCaskill and raises lamb, pork, beef and goat naturally. The fully operational farm doubles as a bed and breakfast, offering guests a glimpse into the quaintness of farm life during their comfortable stay. After a well-rested night in one of the four beautifully decorated rooms, your simple, fresh breakfast can be taken in the antique-laden, country kitchen or on the pergola-covered porch that overlooks the pond and the barn. Old McCaskill's Farm offers a farm-to-table breakfast that includes bacon, eggs, and sausage, all raised here on the farm. On Fridays, you can enjoy a homemade lunch. Life on the farm is hectic but amazingly rewarding.

Call the B&B for Reservations

French Toast Casserole

1 (20-inch) loaf French bread
8 large eggs
2 cups half-and-half
1 cup milk
2 tablespoons sugar
1 teaspoon vanilla extract
¼ teaspoon ground cinnamon
¼ teaspoon ground nutmeg
¼ teaspoon salt

Slice French bread into 20 (1-inch-thick) slices; arrange in 2 rows in a generously greased 9x13-inch baking dish, overlapping slices. In a large bowl, combine eggs, half-and-half, milk, sugar, vanilla, cinnamon, nutmeg and salt; beat until smooth. Pour egg mixture over bread slices, making sure all are coated evenly. Ensure that the mixture gets between slices. Cover with foil and refrigerate overnight. Next day, preheat oven to 350°.

Praline Topping:

2 sticks butter, softened
1 cup packed brown sugar
1 cup chopped pecans
½ teaspoon ground cinnamon
½ teaspoon ground nutmeg

In a bowl, mix all ingredients. Remove foil from casserole dish, top slices with Praline Topping and bake 40 minutes or until puffy and lightly browned.

Restaurant Recipe

Molasses Cookies

¾ cup shortening
1 cup packed brown sugar
1 egg
¼ cup molasses
2¼ cups flour
¼ teaspoon salt
2 teaspoon baking soda
1 teaspoon cinnamon
½ teaspoon ground ginger
Sugar for sprinkling

Preheat oven to 350°. In a bowl, mix all ingredients except sugar together. With greased hands, break off dough and roll into 1-inch balls. Arrange on a greased cookie sheet, 2 inches apart. Sprinkle a cookie with sugar and flatten with the bottom of a glass. Repeat process for each cookie. Bake 12 minutes.

Family Favorite

Laura's Tea Room

105 North Palmer Street
Ridgeway, SC 29130
803-337-8594
www.laurastearoom.com • Find us on Facebook

Located in the small town of Ridgeway, Laura's Tea Room opened its doors in 2008. The Tea Room is housed in a lovely 1911-era building that previously housed the Thomas Company. Tea service is either two or three courses, featuring a selection of hot or iced teas and a three-tiered tray with an assortment of savories and sweets. Located downstairs is a café offering delicious sandwiches, soups, and salads in a relaxing atmosphere. You can even enjoy a pot of hot tea with your lunch. While you wait, browse the gift shop, which carries a range of handcrafted, locally made items and everything tea related. Visit Laura's Tea Room today.

Tuesday – Saturday: 10:00 am to 4:00 pm

Grama's Cornbread Salad

Dressing:

⅔ cup sour cream

⅔ cup mayonnaise

1 (1-ounce) package Hidden Valley
Ranch dressing mix

In a bowl, mix together all ingredients until well combined.

Salad:

1 (8.5-ounce) box Jiffy Corn Muffin
Mix, prepared according to package
directions and crumbled

1 (15-ounce) can pinto beans,
drained and rinsed

½ cup each finely chopped red and
green bell pepper

1 (15.25-ounce) can whole-kernel corn

2 cups shredded Cheddar cheese

In a casserole dish, layer half of each ingredient, except cheese, beginning with cornbread, then beans, then peppers, and finally corn; layer half of prepared dressing. Repeat layering once; top with cheese. Cover and refrigerate overnight. Gently fold together before serving.

Restaurant Recipe

Tearoom Lemon Curd

6 eggs

2 cups sugar

½ cup melted butter

3 regular-size lemons, zested and juiced

In a bowl, beat eggs well. Add sugar, butter, lemon zest and juice; mix well. Transfer mixture to a double boiler over medium-low heat; cook, stirring often, about 30 to 40 minutes, mixing in white foam as it appears. Makes 2 pints. Freeze to keep longer, if desired.

Restaurant Recipe

ARE YOU READY FOR AN OUT OF THIS WORLD DRIVE-BY?

The UFO Welcome Center is a roadside tourist curiosity in Bowman. Though it is not an official tourist attraction, it is great fun to drive by and view the UFO Welcome Center. It will be the highlight of your vacation stories, for sure.

Built in the backyard of Jody Pendarvis, the UFO Welcome Center is a 42-foot-wide flying saucer built out of scrap wood, fiberglass, metal, and random junk. He began building it in 1994, intending it to be a place where aliens could be comfortable meeting people from Earth, later adding a second, smaller saucer on top so that the aliens could take Jody with them when they left.

Inside the 42-foot-wide bottom saucer is a bed, television, air-conditioning unit, shower, and toilet—a friendly place to rest for extraterrestrials who might happen by.

Though it can safely be viewed from the street, it is said that casual visitors are welcome, and Pendarvis is often there to conduct a tour and answer questions about his Willy-Wonka-esque project.

UFO Welcome Center

4004 Homestead Road
Bowman, SC 29018

Enchilada Casserole

2 pounds ground beef

2 (1.5-ounce) packages enchilada seasoning mix

2 (10.25-ounce) cans cream of chicken soup

2 (16-ounce) jars hot or mild picante sauce

4 large corn or flour tortillas

1 (12-ounce) package shredded Cheddar cheese

1 (12-ounce) package shredded mozzarella cheese

Preheat oven to 350°. Brown meat in a skillet over medium heat; drain fat. Add seasoning mix and stir well. Add soup and picante sauce mixing well; heat 2 minutes. Remove from heat and set aside. Line a 9x13-inch casserole dish with 2 tortillas. Layer with half the meat mixture and half the cheeses. Layer remaining 2 tortillas on top of cheese, followed by remaining meat mixture. Bake 30 minutes. Top with remaining cheese. Return to oven just until cheese is melted.

Local Favorite

Buttermilk Biscuits

2 cups all-purpose flour

¼ teaspoon baking soda

2 teaspoons baking powder

2 teaspoons salt

¼ cup Crisco

1 cup buttermilk

Preheat oven to 450°. Grease bottom of a 9x13-inch pan; place in oven to preheat. In a bowl, sift together dry ingredients. Cut Crisco into flour mixture until crumbled. Add buttermilk; mix just until combined. Drop dough in large spoonfuls into preheated pan. Bake 20 minutes, or until golden brown. Makes about 12 biscuits.

Local Favorite

Tuna and Black Olive Melts

2 (6.5 ounce) cans tuna, drained
½ cup finely chopped celery
¼ cup sliced black olives
3 tablespoons chopped red onion
½ cup mayonnaise
⅛ teaspoon pepper
6 English muffins, split
2 tablespoons butter
6 ounces medium-sharp Cheddar
cheese, sliced

Preheat broiler. In a bowl, flake tuna into small chunks; toss with celery, olives and onion. Add mayonnaise; fold until well blended. Season tuna mixture with pepper. Place muffin halves, cut side up, on a baking sheet and lightly toast under broiler. Remove from oven and spread with butter. Evenly divide tuna mixture among muffins and top with cheese. Place back under broiler 5 inches from heat; broil 1 to 2 minutes, or until cheese is melted and bubbly.

Local Favorite

Deviled Crab

⅓ cup vinegar
3 eggs, lightly beaten
1 tablespoon Worcestershire sauce
1 tablespoon butter, melted
1 teaspoon mustard
½ teaspoon celery seed
Salt and pepper to taste
1 cup fresh crabmeat (reserve shells)
1 cup crushed crackers

Preheat oven to 400°. In a saucepan over low heat, mix ⅔ cup water and vinegar; mix in eggs. In a small bowl, mix Worcestershire, butter and mustard; add to saucepan. Add celery seed, salt and pepper; cook until mixture thickens. Stir in crabmeat and cracker crumbs; remove from heat. Spoon mixture into individual shells. Bake 15 to 20 minutes, or until heated through. Serves 6.

Local Favorite

The Little Café

725 South Cherry Road, Suite 180
Rock Hill, SC 29732
803-329-1440
www.thelittlecaferockhill.com • Find us on Facebook

The Little Café is a family restaurant that has been open since 1990. It specializes in down-home cooking at a great price. This charming restaurant also has a buffet on Saturdays and Sundays. The friendly, attentive staff at The Little Café genuinely care about each customer and look forward to you coming back, again and again. Stop by today for Southern-style cooking, meat-and-three, blue plate specials, and food like your mama would cook.

Sunday & Monday: 7:00 am to 3:00 pm
Tuesday – Saturday: 7:00 am to 8:00 pm

Mexican Cornbread

1 cup cornmeal
1 teaspoon baking powder
1 teaspoon salt
½ teaspoon baking soda
½ pound grated cheese
2 tablespoons flour
1 medium onion, grated
3 hot peppers, chopped
¼ cup oil
1 cup milk
2 eggs
1 (8.25-ounce) can cream-style corn

Preheat oven to 450°. In a large bowl, mix together all ingredients; pour into a cast-iron skillet. Bake 30 minutes.

Local Favorite

Willie Sue's Food & Spirits

3355 Patriot Parkway
Sumter, SC 29154
803-469-2500
Find us on Facebook

Willie Sue's Food & Spirits was opened in November 2014 by Sumter native Ricky McLeod. He named it after Grandmother Willie Sue McLeod. The use of reclaimed wood from Sumter's old railroad station as well as historical pictures of Sumter create an ambiance reminiscent of simpler days. The vast menu consists of appetizers, salads, sandwiches, seafood, steak, ribs, and chicken. The steaks are cooked to perfection on a one-of-a-kind wood grill. Complete with flat-screen TVs, the bar boasts one of the largest bourbon selections in South Carolina, ice-cold draft beers, and many specialty drinks. The restaurant also has a heated/cooled outdoor patio for accommodating large parties.

Monday – Thursday:
11:00 am to 10:00 pm
Friday & Saturday: 11:00 am to 11:00 pm
Sunday: 11:00 am to 10:00 pm

Shrimp & Grits

32 ounces chicken broth

1 cup grits

2 cups heavy cream

1 (8-ounce) bag shredded mild Cheddar cheese

1 tablespoon olive oil

4 ounces country ham, chopped

12 ounces andouille sausage, chopped

1 bunch green onions, sliced

1 each red, orange and yellow bell peppers, diced

2 ounces Texas Pete Buffalo Wing sauce

1 (8-ounce) pack sliced portabella mushrooms

1 pound jumbo shrimp, peeled and deveined

Bring broth to a boil; slowly whisk in grits to avoid clumps. Reduce to low heat, stirring often. Once thickened, add heavy cream and stir in cheese; set aside. Using a large skillet over medium heat, heat oil. Sauté ham and sausage 4 to 5 minutes. Add onions, peppers, wing sauce and mushrooms; cover pan. Cook 5 to 7 minutes, stirring occasionally, until pepper-onion mixture is tender and translucent. Add shrimp and cook 3 minutes, or until shrimp are pink and heated through. Place grits in a bowl and spoon sauce over top. Enjoy.

Restaurant Recipe

CAFÉ STRUDEL

— Since 1997 —

Restaurant   Bar   Cafe

300 State St. W.Columbia, SC

Café Strudel

300 State Street
West Columbia, SC 29169
803-794-6634

309 South Lake Drive
Lexington, SC 29072

www.cafestrudel.com • Find us on Facebook

Welcome to Café Strudel, located in the historic Mill Village neighborhood of West Columbia. Famous for its Hangover Hash Browns and awesome Sunday brunch, this cozy café is a favorite of locals and tourists alike. Stop in for great food and maybe a Bloody Mary made with bacon-infused vodka. The staff strive to serve the freshest, most delicious fare possible and to create a memorable dining experience, all for a reasonable price. The Café sources locally, participates in the community, and utilizes eco-friendly practices where feasible. The Café Strudel family looks forward to your visit. It's all about the food.

Monday & Tuesday: 8:00 am to 3:00 pm
Wednesday & Thursday: 8:00 am to 9:00 pm
Friday & Saturday: 8:00 am to 10:00 pm
Sunday: 10:00 am to 9:00 pm

Congaree Chicken Salad

2½ pounds chicken breast, cooked,
shredded or diced

2¼ cups mayonnaise

1 cup relish

1½ tablespoons celery seed

1 tablespoon onion powder

1 tablespoon garlic powder

1½ teaspoons salt

½ teaspoon ground black pepper

¾ cup dried cranberries

¾ cup chopped pecans

¼ cup yellow curry powder

In a large bowl, mix all ingredients together until well combined. Chill at least 1 hour before serving. Yields approximately 2 quarts.

Restaurant Recipe

Horseradish Pimento Cheese

5 cups shredded Cheddar cheese

½ cup diced pimentos

¼ cup grated yellow onion

¼ cup softened cream cheese

6 tablespoons horseradish

¼ cup mayonnaise

1½ teaspoons salt

In a large bowl, mix together all ingredients until well combined. Refrigerate at least 1 hour before serving. Yields approximately 1½ quarts.

Restaurant Recipe

THE *Market* RESTAURANT

322 Little Brooke Lane
West Columbia, SC 29172
803-509-5641
Find us on Facebook

The Market Restaurant is a locally owned restaurant at the State Farmers Market, serving the finest South Carolina cuisine. Recognizing the superior quality and taste that fresh, local products provide, The Market Restaurant has dedicated itself to providing customers with fresh products and produce from the Farmers Market. Menu items are scratch-made and come at affordable prices. Inside, you'll also find The Market Tea Room, which offers full tea service as well as South Carolina products and local artisan wares for purchase. Outside, The Market Seafood shed offers a variety of fresh-caught coastal seafood available raw, steamed, or fried; local favorites like Lowcountry boil; and specialty items like crab dip.

Monday – Saturday: 7:00 am to 2:30 pm

Crab Salad

1 pound lump crabmeat
½ teaspoon each minced garlic, Cajun seasoning, and Old Bay Seasoning
¼ cup diced celery
¼ cup diced red bell pepper
¼ cup diced purple onion
Half a lemon, juiced
2 to 3 ounces mayonnaise

In a large bowl, mix all ingredients until well combined.

Seafood Shed Recipe

Famous Market Burger

6 ounces fresh ground beef
Salt and pepper to taste
1 teaspoon Montreal steak seasoning
2 slices bacon
1 teaspoon butter
1 brioche bun
1 egg
1 slice white American cheese
1 slice deli ham
1 leaf lettuce
1 slice tomato

While grill preheats, season beef with salt and pepper to taste and form into a patty. Sprinkle each side with steak seasoning and cook to desired internal temperature (160° to 165° for a well-done burger). Meanwhile, add bacon to grill, cooking until crisp. Butter bun and toast on grill. Fry egg over easy. Melt cheese over patty. Warm ham on grill. To assemble burger, place patty with melted cheese on bottom bun; top with bacon, egg, ham, lettuce, tomato and top bun. Enjoy.

Restaurant Recipe

South Carolina Benedictine

1 large South Carolina cucumber
1 small South Carolina white onion
½ teaspoon salt, divided
½ cup cream cheese, softened
½ cup sour cream
¼ cup loosely packed fresh dill
1 tablespoon local honey

Purée cucumber, onion and ¼ teaspoon salt in a blender. Using a double-layered cheesecloth, squeeze as much liquid as possible from mixture; discard liquid. Using blender again, blend cream cheese, sour cream, dill, honey and remaining salt until smooth. Stir in cucumber-onion mixture. Serve with crackers for dipping or use as a filling for tea sandwiches.

Tea Room Recipe

Road Runner Café

1153 Kincaid Bridge Road
Winnsboro, SC 29180
803-635-1600
www.roadrunnercafesc.com
Find us on Facebook

Established over thirty years ago, Road Runner Café is a local favorite known for its famous "Mean Gene" burger. Now under new ownership, this Winnsboro staple is ready to serve everyone's favorite comfort food on the road. Enjoy savory burgers, crispy chicken wings, fresh salads, and much more. Pair your meal with your choice of raw, home-style, or crinkle-cut fries dressed with seasoned salt or malt vinegar. Desserts like cake and pie will satisfy your sweet tooth. Quench your thirst with a refreshing glass of sweet tea as you enjoy your dish. The Café also accepts take-out orders for diners on the go. Drop by the Road Runner Café today.

Monday – Thursday & Saturday:
7:00 am to 7:30 pm
Friday: 7:00 am to 9:00 pm

Mountain Dew Cake

1 (12-ounce) can Mountain Dew, divided
1 box lemon cake mix
**1 (3.4-ounce) box instant
lemon pudding mix**
4 eggs
¾ cup canola oil

Preheat oven to 350°. Grease and flour a 9x13-inch baking pan; set aside. In a large bowl, combine 1 cup Mountain Dew with remaining ingredients. Using a hand mixer on low speed, mix batter just until moistened. Increase speed to medium; beat 2 minutes. Pour batter into pan. Bake 45 minutes, or until toothpick inserted into center comes out clean. While cake is baking, make icing.

Icing:

2 cups powdered sugar

In a bowl, combine sugar with remaining Mountain Dew, mixing until smooth. When cake is baked, remove from oven; immediately poke holes in cake with a fork. Pour icing over cake. Enjoy.

Restaurant Recipe

Skillet Popover

1 tablespoon cinnamon
1 tablespoon sugar
½ cup butter
½ cup milk
½ cup all-purpose flour
2 eggs

Preheat oven to 475°. In a small bowl, mix together cinnamon and sugar; set aside. Place butter in a heavy 9-inch iron skillet. Place pan in oven. In a mixing bowl, blend milk, flour and eggs lightly to make batter. After the butter has melted, tilt pan so that the entire surface will be coated with butter. Add batter and bake 12 minutes. Remove from oven and invert onto a large plate. Drizzle butter in pan over popover. Sprinkle with cinnamon sugar. Roll over in loose jelly roll fashion. Slice and serve.

Local Favorite

Vegetable Tempura

2 cups all-purpose flour
2 teaspoons salt
2 teaspoons paprika
2 tablespoons oil
1 tablespoon dry sherry
Vegetables of choice, thickly julienned

Preheat oil in deep fryer to 350°. In a large bowl, mix all ingredients except vegetables with 1¾ cups water. Dip vegetables in batter and fry until golden brown. Drain on paper towels and enjoy.

Local Favorite

Shrimp and Grits Hushpuppies

1½ cups all-purpose flour

1½ cups cornmeal

2 tablespoons baking powder

2 tablespoons sugar

1 tablespoon baking soda

2 teaspoons kosher salt

½ teaspoon cayenne

1 yellow onion, grated

1¼ cups buttermilk

2 large eggs, beaten

1 pound raw shrimp, peeled, deveined and minced

2 cups shredded sharp Cheddar cheese

Canola oil for frying

Hot sauce for serving

Tartar sauce for serving

In a large mixing bowl, whisk together flour, cornmeal, baking powder, sugar, baking soda, salt and cayenne. Add onion, buttermilk and eggs; mix until blended. Stir in shrimp and cheese until just combined. Pour oil to a depth of 2 inches in a deep fryer or heavy pot over medium high heat or until a deep fry thermometer reads 375°. Using a tablespoon, drop small rounds of batter into the oil, making sure not to crowd the pan. Dip the spoon into a glass of water after each hushpuppy is dropped in the oil. Cook stirring occasionally, until golden, about 3 to 4 minutes. Remove hushpuppies and drain on paper towels.

Local Favorite

Tropical Dip

1 (8-ounce) can crushed pineapple, drained

1 (3.4-ounce) package instant vanilla pudding mix

¾ cup cold milk

½ cup flaked coconut

½ cup sour cream

Toasted coconut

Fresh fruit of your choice

In a blender, combine pineapple, pudding, milk, coconut and sour cream; process 30 seconds. Transfer to serving bowl; cover and chill 30 minutes. Garnish with toasted coconut. Serve with fruit.

Local Favorite

Pee Dee

The River's Edge

Restaurant

162 Second Street
Cheraw, SC 29520
843-537-1109
www.theriversedgecheraw.com • Find us on Facebook

Nestled in the historic district of Cheraw, which General Sherman once called "the prettiest town in Dixie," is a family-owned restaurant and bakery—The River's Edge Restaurant. It is the River's Edge staff's delight to serve quality food made from family recipes passed down through generations. Comforting entrées are followed by a large selection of scratch-made desserts, which customers describe as "a bit of heaven." A customer favorite is the Toasted Coconut–Caramel Pecan Cream Cheese Pie. Besides a full menu, there is a featured special each day, such as roast beef and meatloaf just like mom used to make. On Thursday and Friday evenings, you can enjoy grilled steaks, smoked Boston butts, and ribs. "Come sit around Our table!"

Lunch:
Monday – Friday: 10:30 am to 2:30 pm
Dinner:
Thursday & Friday: 5:00 pm to 8:30 pm

Wedding Potatoes

Enjoy this traditional recipe served at weddings.

⅔ cup shredded Cheddar cheese
1⅔ cups half-and-half
1¼ teaspoons salt
1 teaspoon black pepper
1 (16-ounce) container sour cream
1 (10.5-ounce) can cream of chicken soup
¼ cup chopped green bell pepper
1 tablespoon onion flakes
6 white potatoes, shredded and sautéed

Preheat oven to 350°. In a medium bowl, mix all ingredients except potatoes. Fold in potatoes. Transfer mixture to a greased 9x13-inch pan. Cover and bake 45 minutes.

Restaurant Recipe

Lemon Icebox Pie

This is a perfect, refreshing summer dessert.

1½ cups melted margarine
1 cup sugar
3½ cups crushed graham crackers
3½ cups powdered sugar
2 (8-ounce) packages cream cheese, softened
2 (8-ounce) containers Cool Whip
2½ cups sweetened condensed milk
1 cup lemon juice
¼ teaspoon yellow food coloring

Preheat oven to 350°. In a bowl, mix margarine, sugar and graham crackers until well combined. Pat mixture into a 10x15-inch pan. Bake 7 minutes, then remove from oven to cool. In a bowl, beat together powdered sugar and cream cheese until smooth. Fold in Cool Whip. Spread into cooled crust. In bowl of a stand mixer, combine remaining ingredients; beat 15 minutes. Spread over top of pie. Enjoy.

Restaurant Recipe

Beef and Potatoes Casserole

1½ pounds ground beef
Salt, pepper and seasoned salt to taste
6 potatoes, thinly sliced
2 onions, thinly sliced
2 (14.5-ounce) cans crushed tomatoes

Preheat oven to 350°. Brown ground beef in a skillet over medium-high heat; season to taste. Treat a 9x13-inch baking pan with nonstick spray. Layer about half the potatoes in bottom of pan; season with salt and pepper to taste. Layer onions, tomatoes and ground beef, using about half of each; repeat layers, seasoning potatoes with salt and pepper. Bake 1 hour.

Local Favorite

Grilled Vegetarian Stuffed Peppers

4 assorted bell peppers, halved and seeded
6 tablespoons extra virgin olive oil, divided (plus extra for drizzling)
1 cup thinly sliced shallots
Kosher salt and fresh ground black pepper
1⅓ cups chopped tomatoes
⅓ cup golden raisins
1 cup couscous
1 cup chopped fresh parsley
1 cup crumbled feta cheese
1 large egg, beaten
Mixed greens

Heat grill to medium high. Drizzle peppers with 2 tablespoons oil. Grill 10 to 12 minutes, or until charred in spots. While peppers are grilling, combine 3 tablespoons oil, shallots and a pinch of salt in a large cast iron skillet, place on grill and cook 5 minutes stirring often or until shallots soften. Add tomatoes and raisins: cook 1 minute. Add couscous and 1½ cups water, season to taste with salt and pepper. Simmer 4 minutes, stirring constantly or until water has evaporated. Remove from heat, place in a bowl and set aside to cool.

Local Favorite

Charleston Red Rice

2 cups uncooked long-grain white rice
1 tablespoon salt
6 slices bacon
2 onions, chopped
1 (8-ounce) can tomato sauce
1 (6-ounce) can tomato paste
1 tablespoon sugar
2 teaspoons Worcestershire sauce
1 dash hot pepper sauce

Preheat oven to 325°. Grease a 2-quart baking dish. Bring rice, 6 cups water and salt to a boil. Reduce heat to medium-low, cover; simmer until rice is tender and most of the liquid has been absorbed, 20 to 25 minutes. While rice is boiling, cook bacon in a large, deep skillet over medium-high heat until evenly browned, about 10 minutes. Remove bacon and crumble. Reserve about 1 tablespoon bacon drippings in pan. Reduce heat to medium. Cook onions in reserved bacon drippings until translucent, 5 to 8 minutes. Stir in crumbled bacon, tomato sauce, tomato paste, sugar, Worcestershire sauce and hot sauce. Bring mixture to a simmer, reduce heat, and simmer 10 minutes. Spoon cooked rice into prepared baking dish and stir in tomato-bacon mixture until evenly combined. Cover dish and bake in preheated oven 45 minutes.

Local Favorite

Shrimp and Corn Pie

1 (15-ounce) can whole kernel corn
2 eggs, lightly beaten
1 tablespoon butter, melted
½ cup milk
1 cup cooked shrimp
1 teaspoon Worcestershire
Salt, pepper and mace to taste

Preheat oven to 300°. In a bowl, combine all ingredients. Bake in buttered 1-quart casserole dish for 30 minutes. Serves 6.

Local Favorite

The Shed Restaurant

116 Second Street
Cheraw, SC 29520
843-253-5282
Find us on Facebook

The Shed Restaurant is located in the historic district of Cheraw, just steps from Old St. David Church, which was used as a hospital during the Civil War. The Shed Restaurant is a country buffet serving authentic, homemade Southern cuisine, like mac and cheese, collards, stewed beef and rice, pork chops, fried chicken, meatloaf, chicken and dumplings, biscuits, cornbread fritters, banana pudding, and peach cobbler just to name a few. They also offer a full salad bar. Stop by when you're in town or call in to see what's on the hot bar today.

Tuesday – Friday: 11:00 am to 2:00 pm
Sunday: 11:00 am to 2:30 pm

Thirty-Day Slaw

Dressing:

1 cup white vinegar
½ cup extra-virgin olive oil
1 teaspoon celery seed
1 teaspoon mustard seed
1½ cups sugar
1 tablespoon salt

In a saucepan over medium-high heat, mix all ingredients and, stirring constantly, bring to a boil. Remove from heat and stir; set aside to cool.

1 cabbage, grated
1 red bell pepper, diced
1 green bell pepper, diced
2 onions, diced

Toss together in a bowl. Add to cooled Dressing and refrigerate 24 hours before serving.

Restaurant Recipe

Sweet Potato Casserole

4 cups boiled, mashed sweet potatoes
1 cup sugar
1 teaspoon vanilla extract
1 stick butter, softened
2 eggs, beaten
Dash salt

Preheat oven to 350°. Mix all ingredients together in a bowl. Pour into a 9x13-inch casserole dish.

Topping:

1 cup packed brown sugar
1 cup chopped pecans
1 cup flaked coconut
1 stick butter, melted
¼ cup self-rising flour

Mix all ingredients in a bowl. Pour over top of Sweet Potato Casserole and bake 30 minutes. Serves 8.

Restaurant Recipe

Wholly Smokin' Downtown

BBQ, Ribs & a WHOLE lot more!

150 South Dargan Street
Florence, SC 29506
843-407-7545
www.whollysmokinbbq.com • Find us on Facebook, Instagram & Twitter @whollysmokin

Wholly Smokin' was founded in 2012 by Bill Travis. After twenty-five years in the jewelry industry, he turned his hobby and passion of smoking meats into a restaurant business. Having placed in several barbecue competitions, Wholly Smokin' quickly received recognition from friends and barbecue enthusiasts statewide. In 2014, Bill and his wife, Jackie, partnered with friends Andy and Christina Jeffords and moved the restaurant to downtown Florence's historic district. The restaurant has since been placed on the SC BBQ Trail, the Pecan Trail, and named in the top 10 barbecue joints in South Carolina. Wholly Smokin' looks forward welcoming you. At Wholly Smokin', customers become friends and friends become family.

Tuesday – Thursday: 11:00 am to 9:00 pm
Friday & Saturday: 11:00 am to 10:00 pm
Sunday: 11:00 am to 8:00 pm

Warm Goat Cheese Salad

⅓ cup shredded Parmesan cheese
2 ounces goat cheese, softened
⅓ cup chopped pecans
½ to 2 cups mixed spring greens
6 cherry tomatoes, halved
1 small cucumber, sliced
¼ cup chopped red onion
2 dozen pecan halves
Oil for frying

Preheat oven to 325°. To make cheese crisp, place Parmesan on a baking sheet lined with a Silpat. Bake 12 to 15 minutes; cool before removing from sheet. Form goat cheese into a patty and coat in chopped pecans; chill 1 hour. Arrange greens, tomatoes, cucumber, onion and pecan halves in a salad bowl; set aside. Heat oil in a skillet over low heat. Place goat cheese patty in skillet and cook 2 minutes on each side. Top salad with patty and Parmesan crisp. Pair with dressing of choice (we use a house-made raspberry vinaigrette).

Courtesy of Chef Bill Harwell
Restaurant Recipe

Bill's Smokin' Chili

2 tablespoons minced garlic
2 large onions, chopped
3 stalks celery, diced
1 jalapeño pepper, diced
1 tablespoon oregano
3 pounds chuck roast
(or other meat of choice), diced
Salt to taste
¼ cup chili powder
1 (28-ounce) can diced tomatoes
1 (6-ounce) can tomato paste
2 (16-ounce) cans tomato sauce
1 (14-ounce) can crushed tomatoes
1 (20-ounce) can light chili beans
1 (20-ounce) can dark chili beans

In a stockpot over medium-high heat, add garlic, onions, celery, jalapeño, oregano and meat; cook 5 to 7 minutes or until vegetables are soft. Add remaining ingredients plus 4½ cups water to pot. Reduce heat to low and simmer at least 3 hours.

Restaurant Recipe

NUCLEAR BOMB ATTACK IN SOUTH CAROLINA?

Well, it wasn't exactly an attack, but there certainly was a bomb dropped here. The atom bomb was developed near the end of World War II. Due to a very odd accident, one was actually dropped in Mars Bluff on March 11, 1958.

An Air Force B-47 Stratojet took off from Hunter Air Force Base, carrying nuclear weapons on board in the event of war with the Soviet Union. After a fault light indicated the bomb harness locking pin did not engage, Air Force Captain Bruce Kulka was summoned to investigate. As he reached around the bomb to pull himself up, he mistakenly grabbed the emergency release pin. The Mark 6 nuclear bomb dropped to the floor of the B-47, and the weight forced the bomb bay doors open, sending the bomb 15,000 feet down to the ground below. It landed in the backyard of Walter Gregg and his family.

If you can call being bombed by your own country "lucky," it was at least fortunate that the fissile nuclear core was still secured on the jet. However, 7,600 pounds of conventional high explosives detonated, transforming the Greggs' vegetable garden into a crater 75 feet wide and 30 feet deep. The bomb's detonation leveled nearby pine trees, totaled both of Gregg's vehicles, and virtually destroyed his residence, leaving the home in ruin. Amazingly, Gregg and his family suffered only minor injuries.

Gregg later sold the property, and the plot of land where the crater was located passed through several owners. The crater is still present today, although fifty years of vegetation has reduced the formerly impressive pit to a 40-foot-wide, leafy depression in the woods. On the 50th anniversary of the accident, a state historical marker was erected by the highway. Near the crater is a plywood cutout of the bomb and an interpretive storyboard displaying copies of local newspaper stories from 1958.

In addition to visiting the Mars Bluff Crater, be sure to check out artifacts of the amazing incident that are on display in the Florence County Museum's Pee Dee History Gallery.

Mars Bluff Crater

E. Palmetto Street
6.5 miles east of Florence

Florence County Museum

111 West Cheves Street
Florence, SC 29501
843-676-1200
www.flocomuseum.org

Woodstone BBQ & Seafood Restaurant

1247 South Irby Street
Florence, SC 29501
843-629-1290
www.woodstonebbq.com • Find us on Facebook

Opened by Roger and Sheryl Pope in 2008, Woodstone BBQ & Seafood Restaurant is now owned and operated by Jesse & Christi Mills. Serving the Florence area for nearly a decade now, Woodstone's customers know where to come to get their fix. Guests will enjoy barbecue made the old-fashioned way, pulled by hand and dressed with a succulent, vinegar-based sauce. The restaurant also offers a variety of seafood, like fried shrimp and farm-raised catfish, and other Southern favorites, like fried chicken, mac-n-cheese, and sweet potato casserole. Stop in today for down-home cooking and friendly atmosphere.

Thursday: 11:00 am to 8:30 pm
Friday & Saturday: 11:00 am to 9:00 pm
Sunday: 11:00 am to 2:30 pm

Peach Cobbler

4 cups flour
2 cups sugar
½ cup vanilla extract
1 tablespoon cinnamon sugar
1 (6-pound) can sliced peaches
Milk as needed

Preheat oven to 350°. Whisk together flour, sugar, vanilla and cinnamon sugar in a large bowl. Slowly add milk while stirring until mixture is thin enough to pour out of bowl; do not overly thin. Butter a large baking pan; pour in peaches and juice. Pour batter mixture over top until peaches are covered. Bake 25 minutes or until top is golden brown. Serve with vanilla ice cream or enjoy by itself.

Restaurant Recipe

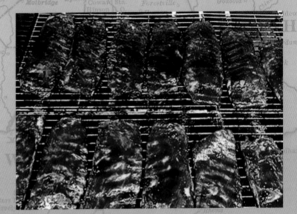

Ball & Que Restaurant

1808 Highmarket Street
Georgetown, SC 29440
843-546-6404
Find us on Facebook

Welcome to the one and only Ball & Que Restaurant, proudly serving the Georgetown area since first opening in 1970. This quaint eatery serves breakfast, lunch, and dinner six days a week. With a rotating menu of daily specials, diners get a different food experience every time they stop by for a bite to eat. Enjoy delicious fried chicken and Ball & Que's famous cheese biscuits. The country-style menu includes Southern favorites like chicken fried steak, chicken and dumplings, macaroni and cheese, coleslaw, peach cobbler, and more.

Monday – Saturday: 6:00 am to 9:00 pm

Grandma Mildred's Coconut Pie

3 cups sugar
6 eggs
1 quart heavy whipping cream
1 tablespoon vanilla extract
21 ounces flaked coconut
1 stick butter, melted
3 (8-inch) pie shells

Preheat oven to 275°. Mix sugar and eggs together in a bowl. Add cream and vanilla; mix well. Add coconut; mix until fully incorporated. Stir in butter. Divide filling evenly between pie shells and bake 2 hours. Enjoy.

Restaurant Recipe

Jeep Ford Salad

Mixed salad greens
Cherry tomatoes, sliced
Cucumbers, peeled and sliced
Shredded Cheddar cheese
Strawberries, sliced
Mandarin orange segments
Dried cranberries
5 to 6 fried chicken tenders
Raspberry vinaigrette dressing
Crackers

In a bowl, toss together greens, tomatoes, cucumbers, cheese, strawberries, oranges and cranberries. Plate and top with chicken tenders. Serve with raspberry vinaigrette and crackers on the side.

Restaurant Recipe

Strawberry Salsa

1 pint ripe strawberries, hulled
and finely diced

2 teaspoons honey

1 jalapeño pepper, seeded
and finely diced

½ cup finely diced red onion

⅔ cup loosely packed chopped
fresh cilantro

Pinch salt and black pepper

Mix all ingredients in a bowl. Refrigerate 30 minutes. Serve with warmed tortilla chips.

Local Favorite

Easy Fudge Pie

2 cups sugar

½ cup cocoa

½ cup self-rising flour

2 sticks margarine, melted

4 eggs, beaten

2 teaspoons vanilla flavoring

1 cup chopped pecans, optional

2 (9-inch) unbaked pie shells

Preheat oven to 325°. In a large mixing bowl, mix all ingredients except pie shells; pour into pie shells. Bake 35 to 40 minutes, or until set in middle; cool completely. Serve with vanilla ice cream.

Local Favorite

Cherry Coke Salad

2 (4-ounce) cans pitted dark
cherries with juice

1 (3ounce) package cherry Jell-O

1 (2-ounce) can crushed
pineapple with juice

1 cup Coca-Cola

½ cup chopped pecans

In a saucepan over medium-high heat, bring cherries and their juice to boiling. Remove from heat: add Jell-O and stir. Add pineapple with juice, coke and nuts. Pour into an oiled 6-cup mold. Let cool, then refrigerate at least 2 hours or until completely set. Serve cold.

Local Favorite

Crab Stuffed Chicken Breasts

Salt and pepper
6 boneless, skinless chicken breasts
½ cup chopped onion
½ cup chopped celery
3 tablespoons butter, plus more for drizzle
3 tablespoons white wine
1 (7-ounce) can crabmeat
½ cup Pepperidge Farm stuffing
2 tablespoons flour
½ teaspoon paprika

Preheat oven to 375°. Salt and pepper chicken breasts. Cut a slit into side of breast to form an envelope for the stuffing; set aside. In a small skillet over medium heat, cook onion and celery in butter until tender. Remove from heat and add wine, crabmeat and stuffing. Insert stuffing into slit in breasts and secure with toothpicks. Combine flour and paprika; dredge stuffed breasts in flour mixture. Place breasts in a baking dish, drizzle with butter and bake uncovered for 40 minutes. Pour sauce over breasts when serving.

Sauce:

1 (1.25-ounce) envelope Hollandaise Sauce Mix
¾ cup milk
2 tablespoons white wine
½ cup shredded Swiss cheese

Heat ingredients and spoon over chicken.

Local Favorite

Sweet Potato Biscuits

1 cup flour
3 teaspoons baking powder
½ teaspoon salt
4 tablespoons shortening
1 cup cooked and mashed sweet potatoes
½ to ¾ cup milk

Preheat oven to 400°. Sift together flour, baking powder and salt. Mix in shortening and sweet potatoes. Add milk until stiff enough to roll out to ½-inch thickness on floured surface. Cut out biscuits and place on buttered pan. Bake 20 to 30 minutes, or until nicely browned.

Local Favorite

Scott's Bar-B-Que

2734 Hemingway Highway
Hemingway, SC 29554
843-558-0134
Find us on Facebook

Scott's Bar-B-Que began as Scott's Variety, an old-fashioned country store, when it was opened in 1972 by Ella and Roosevelt Scott. What began as a weekly family tradition of smoking whole hogs soon became an integral part of the family business. Patrons would travel from miles away to get a taste of the best barbecue around. Scott's smokes their hogs on-site over custom-built wood-burning pits, and even makes their own charcoal. The vinegar-based pepper barbecue sauce ties everything together perfectly, but they still insist on one other secret ingredient: "We put a whole lot of love into what we do." You'll definitely love this Hemingway tradition.

Wednesday: 9:30 am to 5:30 pm
Thursday & Friday: 9:30 am to 8:30 pm
Saturday: 9:30 am to 8:00 pm

Mrs. Ella's Baked Beans

1 (28-ounce) can baked beans

Molasses to taste

Mustard to taste

Brown sugar to taste

Scott's special vinegar-based barbecue sauce to taste

And lots of Love

Preheat oven to 325°. Mix together all ingredients in a large bowl; transfer to a baking dish. Bake uncovered about 2 hours.

Restaurant Recipe

WHAT DO A LUCKY RABBIT'S FOOT, GREEN BEANS AND AN ASTRONAUT HAVE IN COMMON?

Lake City is home to the Bean Market building, a bronze statue of Huey Cooper and his lucky rabbit's foot, and the statue and tomb of Dr. Ronald E. McNair, who died aboard the Space Shuttle *Challenger*.

On January 28, 1986, Dr. Ronald E. McNair was on the Space Shuttle *Challenger*, which disintegrated shortly after takeoff, killing him and six other crew members. A renowned research scientist, Dr. McNair flew his first mission on the *Challenger* in 1984. There is now a park named for McNair that includes a mausoleum and statue of the hometown astronaut, who is a Lake City local hero. Adjacent to the park, the Dr. Ronald E. McNair Life History Center is housed in the same building that was the Lake City Public Library in 1959, when McNair, then 9 years old, refused to leave the library after being told he could not check out books.

Built in 1936 by the Public Works Administration (PWA), as part of Franklin Delano Roosevelt's "New Deal," the Lake City bean market rose to acclaim as the world's largest truck auction of green beans. Farmers drove to Lake City from all over the South to bring their bean crops to market; traders would then ship the beans north on freight trains. Today, in addition to providing a link to the past, the Bean Market building is a community civic center and is listed on the National Register of Historic Places.

In the 1960s, Huey Cooper was a fixture in downtown Lake City for as long as anyone could remember. He lived rent-free in a small building built and paid for by the police department. He was always cheerful and spent most days on a low, cement wall at the corner of Acline and Main Streets, where passers-by could rub his lucky rabbit's foot for a nickel. Huey would use his income to buy cigars and bottled Coke at the nearby train depot. Huey claimed to have been born in 1873, which would have made him 105 when he died in 1978. Years later, a statue was commissioned to preserve Huey's legacy. The bronze statue sculpted by Alex Palkovich was unveiled September 2014, forever holding out his rabbit's foot. There is even a slot in his right pocket for luck-seekers to deposit their nickels.

Ronald E. McNair Life History Center

235 East Main Street
Lake City, SC 29560
843-374-0046

Bean Market

111 Henry Street
Lake City, SC 29560
843-374-1500

Huey Cooper Statue

Corner of Acline and Main Street
Lake City, SC 29560

www.lakecitysc.com

Shrimper of Lake City

340 West Main Street
Lake City, SC 29560
843-374-2063
www.lakecityshrimper.placeweb.site

The Shrimper of Lake City serves up all of your seafood favorites in an old-fashioned fish house atmosphere. Guests will enjoy seafood classics like shrimp, oysters, crab, and fried catfish. With so many mouth-watering options, the combo dinner is the best way to get a taste of everything. If seafood isn't your thing, the team at the Shrimper has you covered. In addition to fried chicken, guests can also choose from a variety of grilled dishes like hamburger steaks, rib-eye steaks, chicken breasts, and pork chops. Add on a side of fries or a steaming baked potato and you're in for a classic Lake City dining experience.

Sunday – Thursday: 11:00 am to 9:00 pm
Friday & Saturday: 11:00 am to 10:00 pm

Catfish Stew

Catfish
Fatback
Onions
Bell peppers
Tomato juice
Tomato soup
V8 juice
Ketchup
Hot sauce

Here are all the ingredients for the Shrimper of Lake City's famous Catfish Stew. The amounts are secret, so you'll have to figure out the rest on your own. Have fun!

Restaurant Recipe

Chicken Salad

20 pounds chicken, cooked and chopped
25 eggs, hard boiled and chopped
2 cups dry onions
2 bundles celery, finely chopped
½ gallon sweet relish
2 tablespoons white pepper
1 gallon mayonnaise

Mix all ingredients together until well combined. Be careful not to overmix.

Restaurant Recipe

Spiced Applesauce Bread

1 cup chunky applesauce
1 cup sugar
½ cup vegetable oil
2 eggs, beaten
3 tablespoon milk
2 cups flour
1 teaspoon baking soda
½ teaspoon baking powder
¼ teaspoon salt
½ teaspoon nutmeg
¼ teaspoon allspice
½ teaspoon cinnamon, divided
¾ cup chopped pecans, divided
¼ cup brown sugar
½ teaspoon cinnamon

Preheat oven to 350°. In a large mixing bowl, combine applesauce, sugar, oil, eggs and milk well. Add flour, baking soda, baking powder, salt, nutmeg, allspice, ½ teaspoon cinnamon and ½ cup chopped pecans. Mix well and pour into a greased 9-inch loaf pan. In another bowl, combine brown sugar, remaining ½ teaspoon cinnamon and remaining ¼ cup pecans to form topping. Sprinkle over and lightly press into batter. Bake 1 hour or until done.

Local Favorite

Squash and Onions

2 tablespoons butter or olive oil
5 medium yellow squash, sliced
½ medium sweet onion, diced
Salt and pepper to taste

Melt butter over medium-low heat in a skillet. Add squash and onions and cook until onions are translucent and squash is tender, about 8 to 10 minutes. Remove from heat; add salt and pepper to taste. Serve warm.

Local Favorite

Spinach Lasagne

½ pound fresh spinach
1 onion, chopped
1 garlic clove, minced
1 tablespoon olive oil
1 cup cottage cheese
1 egg, beaten
Salt and pepper to taste
1 teaspoon chopped basil
½ teaspoon oregano
2 tablespoons chopped parsley
½ pound lasagna noodles
½ pound mozzarella
cheese, coarsely grated
3 cups tomato sauce

Preheat oven to 350°. Wash spinach, tearing out stems and coarsely chop. Sauté onion and garlic in oil. Combine with spinach, cottage cheese and egg; mix well. Season with salt, pepper, basil, oregano and parsley; set aside. Cook lasagna noodles in boiling salt water until tender. In a buttered 9x13-inch baking dish, layer noodles, cottage cheese mixture, cheese and tomato sauce. Repeat layering 3 times, making sure to end with tomato sauce on top. Cover with aluminum foil and bake 40 minutes. Remove foil and bake an additional 10 minutes.

Local Favorite

Caramel Pound Cake

Cake:

2 sticks butter
½ cup Crisco
3 cups sugar
6 eggs
4 cups all-purpose flour
½ teaspoon baking powder
1 cup milk
1 teaspoon vanilla extract

In a large bowl, cream together butter, Crisco and sugar. Add eggs one at a time to butter mixture. In another bowl, mix flour and baking powder; add to butter mixture. Add milk and vanilla; mix well. Bake at 300° in a well-greased and floured tube pan for 1½ hours, or until cake springs back.

Caramel Icing:

1 stick butter
1 cup brown sugar
¼ cup milk
2 cups powdered sugar
½ teaspoon vanilla extract

In a saucepan, melt butter and brown sugar until bubbly; stir. Add milk. Remove from heat, add powdered sugar and beat with a mixer. Add vanilla and mix well; spread on cooled cake.

Local Favorite

Raspberries & Thyme

329 North Main Street
Marion, SC 29571
843-245-2246
Find us on Facebook

Opened March 2017 in downtown Marion, Raspberries & Thyme is the fruition of nearly four years of painstaking attention to detail. This charming little café is the brainchild of Maggie McCullough and Bob George, two individuals who combined talents to create its curious yet comforting atmosphere. Maggie and Bob craft artisanal experiences using only fresh produce, Boar's Head meats and cheeses, and scratch-made desserts, breads, and salad dressings. For Bob and Maggie, Raspberries & Thyme is the perfect opportunity to introduce the community to a palatable art form that will delight the senses and inspire a return visit for the next "canvas."

Monday – Thursday: 8:00 am to 2:00 pm

Quiche Lorraine

4 eggs, 1 separated
1 (9-inch) pie shell
4 ounces bacon, cooked and drained
1½ cups heavy cream
½ teaspoon salt
¼ teaspoon black pepper

Preheat oven to 375°. In a bowl, beat yolk of 1 egg. Brush pie shell with yolk and bake just until edges begin to brown, about 6 to 8 minutes. Cut up bacon and place in bottom of pie shell. In a large bowl, beat together remaining eggs, heavy cream, salt and black pepper. Pour custard into pie shell. Bake until custard is browned and set, about 25 to 35 minutes.

Restaurant Recipe

Chocolate Chip Cookies

1¼ cup all-purpose flour
½ teaspoon baking soda
1 stick unsalted butter, softened
½ cup sugar
½ cup packed light brown sugar
1 large egg
¼ teaspoon salt
1½ teaspoons vanilla
1 cup semisweet chocolate chips

Preheat oven to 375°. In a bowl, whisk together flour and baking soda; set aside. In a stand mixer on medium speed, beat butter, sugar and brown sugar until fluffy. Add egg, salt and vanilla; beat until well combined. Remove mixing bowl from stand mixer and add flour mixture; stir until smooth. Stir in chocolate chips. Drop heaping teaspoons of dough about 2 inches apart onto a baking sheet lined with parchment paper. Bake, 1 sheet at a time, in center of oven until edges turn brown, about 8 to 10 minutes (for more even browning, turn sheet halfway through cooking). Cool before removing from sheet. Repeat until dough is gone.

Restaurant Recipe

WINTER CASTLE WITH BEAR CAGES?

Atalaya Castle was built by New York philanthropist Archer Huntington, and his wife, Anna, between 1931 and 1933. Archer designed the house as a winter residence after his wife was diagnosed with tuberculosis. Anna, an artist and sculptor, kept bears, horses, monkeys, and even a leopard in animal enclosures on the property, using them as models for her work.

Atalaya, which means "watchtower" in Spanish, was situated on the ocean within an estate that originally consisted of more than 9,000 acres that were previously four rice plantations. The Huntingtons used part of that acreage to build the first public sculpture garden in the United States—Brookgreen Gardens—to showcase Anna's work.

Anna worked in aluminum and bronze, creating hauntingly beautiful statues. With massive indoor and outdoor studios, the mansion had plenty of room for Huntington's work and dozens of rooms for their servants. Surprisingly, however, there are no extra bedrooms, no massive entry hall, no drawing rooms, and no grand dining rooms. There's no room for guests, and the Huntingtons obviously wanted it that way.

After allowing the United States Air Corps to use their home as barracks during World War II, the Huntington's returned to Atalaya in 1946 and 1947. Anna's studio was moved to another portion of the property in Brookgreen Gardens, and the rest of the furnishings that weren't donated elsewhere were sent to Connecticut after the death of Archer in 1955.

In 1960, 2,500 acres of the former estate, including the house and sculpture garden, were leased for free to the state of South Carolina. The Friends of Huntington Beach State Park offer guided tours of Atalaya and operate the Atalaya Visitor Center with exhibits about the house and the Huntingtons. The annual Atalaya Arts and Crafts Festival is held at the castle each year, in late September.

Atalaya

Huntington Beach State Park
16148 Ocean Highway
Murrells Inlet, SC 29576
843-237-4440
www.southcarolinaparks.com/huntington-beach

Lulu's Cafe

1903 North Ocean Boulevard
Myrtle Beach, SC 29577
843-712-1890
Find us on Facebook

When restaurateur Misty Coan opened Lulu's Café in 2011, she set out to create the embodiment of the coastal spirit and growing business climate of the Grand Strand. Her vision to provide great food in an equally matched environment would prove to be a much needed brunch hotspot for locals and visitors alike. Lulu's atmosphere is fun and beachy, featuring reclaimed wood ceilings and elements of personality that make you feel like you're right at home. Customers are treated like family, and many have been with Misty from the beginning. Meet family and friends to relax, eat some yummy food, and sip a mimosa. Come visit anytime.

Daily: 7:00 am to 2:00 pm

Banana Bread

1¼ cups sugar

1 stick butter, softened

2 eggs

1 ½ cups mashed, ripe bananas
(about 3 to 4)

½ cup buttermilk

1½ teaspoons vanilla extract

2½ cups all-purpose flour

1 teaspoon baking soda

1 teaspoon salt

Set rack to lowest position and preheat oven to 350°. Grease bottoms of 2 (8-inch) loaf pans; set aside. Cream together sugar and butter in a large bowl. Stir in eggs until well blended. Add bananas, buttermilk and vanilla; beat until smooth. Stir in flour, baking soda and salt just until moistened. Pour into loaf pans. Bake 1 hour or until toothpick inserted in center comes out clean (if using 9-inch loaf pans, add 15 minutes to baking time). Remove from oven and cool 10 minutes. Remove loaves from pans and place topside up on wire rack. Cool completely, about 2 hours, before slicing.

Restaurant Recipe

Banana Bread French Toast

2 loaves Banana Bread, sliced to
½-inch thickness

4 to 6 eggs

½ teaspoon vanilla extract

Splash cream

Dash cinnamon

Freshly sliced bananas for garnish

Nuts for garnish

Powder sugar for garnish

Whip cream for garnish

Let sliced Banana Bread sit out overnight (this will help it hold the egg wash). In a bowl, beat eggs; stir in vanilla, cream and cinnamon. Dip Banana Bread slices into egg wash, then transfer to a warm, lightly buttered skillet over medium heat. Cook 3 to 4 minutes each side, flipping only once, until golden brown. Transfer to a serving plate and top with banana slices, nuts, powdered sugar and whip cream. Enjoy.

Restaurant Recipe

Schoolhouse Bar-B-Que

2252 Highway 52
Scranton, SC 29591
843-389-2020
www.schoolhousebbq.com • Find us on Facebook

Located in the friendly town of Scranton, Schoolhouse Bar-B-Que offers traditional Southern cooking in a nostalgic, laid-back atmosphere. This country buffet is housed in a 1930's-era schoolhouse. Serving as a warehouse in its later years, the schoolhouse underwent restoration beginning in 1982. In May 1994, Schoolhouse Bar-B-Que opened for business. Today, it features a reasonably priced, all-you-can-eat buffet with all the desserts and soft-serve ice cream you can eat. Schoolhouse specializes in delicious barbecue, but the buffet also includes a wide variety of other meats and vegetables cooked fresh daily.

Schoolhouse Bar-B-Que is filled once again with laughter, conversation, and even learning. Feel free to come by and remember when.

Thursday – Saturday: 11:00 am to 8:30 pm
Sunday: 11:00 am to 2:00 pm

Bacon-Wrapped Chicken

4 raw chicken tenders
Salt and pepper to taste
Chili powder to taste
2 slices bacon, cut in half crosswise
Brown sugar to taste

Preheat oven to 350°. Wash and dry tenders; season with salt and pepper to taste. Cover in chili powder. Wrap each tender with half a slice bacon. Arrange in a baking pan and top with brown sugar to taste. Bake about 30 minutes. Broil 2 to 3 minutes to crisp bacon.

Restaurant Recipe

Old–Fashioned Roasted Pecans

1 egg white
1 tablespoon water
2¼ cups pecan halves
½ cup sugar
¼ teaspoon salt
1½ teaspoons ground cinnamon

Preheat oven to 225°. Lightly grease baking pan. Combine egg white and water in mixing bowl; beat until fluffy. Fold in pecans and coat evenly. Combine sugar, salt and cinnamon in shaker or cup with a lid. Dust pecans evenly with sugar mixture. Spread nuts over prepared pan. Bake until toasted and fragrant, stirring every 15 minutes for about 1 hour. Cool and store in airtight container.

Local Favorite

Roast Beef Hash

2 tablespoons vegetable oil
½ cup diced onion
4 cups cubed russet potatoes
Salt and pepper to taste
½ teaspoon ground sage
2 (15-ounce) cans beef stock
1½ pounds beef roast, cubed

Using a Dutch oven over medium heat, add 1 tablespoon oil; add onion and sauté. When onion is just turning transparent, add remaining oil. Add potatoes, salt, pepper and sage. Sauté 5 minutes, stirring occasionally to prevent sticking. Stir in beef stock and cook 5 minutes. Reduce heat to medium-low; add meat and simmer 30 minutes longer, stirring occasionally to prevent sticking.

Local Favorite

Taco Casserole

1½ pounds ground beef
1 (1.12 ounce) package
taco seasoning mix
2 (8-ounce) cans tomato sauce
1 (11-ounce) can whole kernel corn
1 cup coarsely crushed tortilla chips
1 cup grated Cheddar cheese

Preheat oven to 400°. In a large skillet over medium heat, brown meat and drain. Stir in seasoning mix, then tomato sauce and corn; mix well. Simmer 5 minutes over low heat. Pour mixture into a 2-quart baking dish. Top with chips and cheese. Bake 10 minutes, or until cheese is melted.

Local Favorite

Mustard Sauce

1¾ cups yellow mustard
1⅛ cups honey
⅔ cup apple cider vinegar
¼ cup ketchup
3 tablespoons brown sugar
1 teaspoon Worcestershire sauce
1 teaspoon hot sauce

Comine all ingredients; stir well. Pour into glass jars and seal. Refrigerate and let flavors blend 24 hours before serving.

Local Favorite

Engagement Dip

2 cups chopped sweet onion
2 cups mayonnaise
2 cups shredded Cheddar cheese

Preheat oven to 350°. Stir onion, mayonnaise and cheese together in casserole dish. Bake until golden and bubbly, about 15 to 20 minutes.

Local Favorite

PEARL OF THE PEE DEE, CASH CROP OR THREE-TIME LOSER?

Three times tobacco has risen to the status of cash crop in South Carolina, only to see a major decline soon after. In the late 1800s, tobacco was called "the pearl of the Pee Dee," due to its economic contributions to the state.

Though early settlers planted tobacco in the 1670s, overproduction in Virginia and Maryland kept leaf prices low, and South Carolinians embraced rice as a more profitable staple. In 1760, tobacco made a comeback in the backcountry. Production peaked at ten million pounds in 1799. Then, with the cotton boom of the early 1800s, tobacco growing had again vanished in The Palmetto State.

South Carolina's most important tobacco period began in the Pee Dee region in the 1880s, when cotton profits fell at the same time a sharp rise in cigarette smoking occurred in the United States and Europe. South Carolina tobacco was highly prized by the Europeans, with almost a million pounds a year exported. Bright leaf crops in the region yielded profits of nearly $150 per acre—ten times the value of cotton. Tobacco put Mullins on the map as the tobacco headquarters of the state, and in the late 1800s and early 1900s, city-block-size warehouses were devoted to tobacco.

By the 1920s, tobacco growers were falling on hard times. Forming a cooperative to strengthen their marketing position with big cigarette manufacturers, farmers raised prices for a few years. However, tobacco prices—and the fortunes of the

Pee Dee—hit a long decline after manufacturers began refusing to buy co-op leaf. After the Great Depression of the 1930s forced many farmers into foreclosure, the Agricultural Adjustment Act (AAA) of 1933 revived the Pee Dee economy by balancing supply with demand. The federal tobacco program became the cornerstone of the Pee Dee economy in the 1950s. South Carolina's leaf production peaked in 1955 at 197 million pounds.

The
South
Carolina
Tobacco
Museum
Mullins

By 1970, however, mounting evidence of smoking-related illness was reducing demand for cigarette tobacco, and at the same time, cigarette manufacturers began fostering tobacco production abroad. From 1974 to 1992 the number of tobacco farms declined by 70 percent. As fewer people smoke today, tobacco production has dropped steadily in the state over the years—14,300 acres in 2015 compared to 114,000 acres in 1950.

Though tobacco farming continues to decline in the area, the South Carolina Tobacco Museum captures the history of tobacco in the Pee Dee region, focusing on the growing of tobacco and rural farm life prior to 1950. Displays include the complete growing cycle and production of tobacco from the field to auction; tobacco-related equipment, including a wagon, a reconstructed pole barn, and blacksmith tools; and other special exhibits.

South Carolina Tobacco Museum

104 Northeast Front Street
Mullins, SC 29574
843-464-8194
www.mullinssc.us/sctobaccomuseum

THE GOLDEN EGG
Best Eggs on the Beach!

Golden Egg Pancake House

415 Highway 17 North
Surfside Beach, SC 29575
843-238-4923
www.goldeneggonline.com • Find us on Facebook

Soon after Hurricane Hugo, Tony's Italian Food was converted to the Golden Egg Pancake House. Spurred by the rise in other pizza chains in the area, Golden Egg was opened with the intent to bring something fresh to the area. More than twenty years later, Golden Egg is still serving great breakfast at affordable prices to local regulars and visitors. Although not as big as other breakfast joints, Golden Egg strives to provide quality food and great service. With a sharp focus on quality, menu items are often changed to reflect the best ingredients available. Visit Golden Egg Pancake House where they take no shortcuts to make great food.

Daily: 6:00 am to 2:00 pm

Pumpkin Pancakes

1 pound buttermilk pancake mix
¾ cup pumpkin pie filling
2 tablespoons packed brown sugar
2 tablespoons pumpkin pie spice
2 tablespoons ground cinnamon
Chopped walnuts (or pecans) for garnish

In a large bowl, prepare pancake mix according to package directions. Mix in remaining ingredients except walnuts, stirring until smooth. Pour batter onto a preheated griddle or pan. Cook 3 minutes or until bubbles appear on surface of pancake; flip and cook other side 2 minutes or until browned. Garnish with nuts if desired. Refrigerate any unused batter up to 5 days.

Restaurant Recipe

Red, White & Blue Waffle

This is a simple recipe honoring our country. Stop by and have one.

Waffle mix plus ingredients to prepare
½ cup sliced fresh strawberries
½ cup fresh blueberries
Whipped cream for topping

Preheat waffle iron. Prepare waffle mix according to directions on box. Spray waffle iron with nonstick spray and drop ¾ cup batter onto iron. Close and cook 5 minutes or until golden brown. Remove waffle from iron and plate it. On one half of waffle, place strawberries, and on the other, place blueberries. Top with whipped cream in middle.

Restaurant Recipe

Lowcountry

Jason's Seafood & Wings

7 Robert Smalls Parkway
Beaufort, SC 29906
843-379-8257
www.jseafoodandwings.com
Find us on Facebook

Chef Jason Cummings has worked as an executive chef with various large corporations and small ventures for over twenty years, gaining the knowledge, spirit, and professionalism necessary to succeed in the restaurant industry. In an effort to put these experiences and skills to practice, Jason opened his own restaurant. At Jason's Seafood & Wings, patrons can expect second-to-none food and beverage service from Chef Jason himself. He puts his personal touch on every dish offered. Chef Jason constantly endeavors to exceed his guests' expectations with world-class cuisine, seamless service, and affordable pricing. Stop by Jason's Seafood & Wings to see what he can do for you.

Monday – Wednesday: 11:00 am to 8:00 pm
Thursday – Saturday: 11:00 am to 9:00 pm

Jason's
Seafood & Wings

Seafood Cake

½ pound tilapia
⅓ cup mayonnaise
2 tablespoons Dijon mustard
1 tablespoon lemon juice
2 tablespoons Old Bay seasoning
1 tablespoon small diced onion
½ cup cooked small shrimp
½ cup panko breadcrumbs
1 pound lump crabmeat

In a saucepan over high heat, bring 3 cups water to a rolling boil; lower heat to a simmer. Add tilapia and cook 5 to 7 minutes, or until able to flake fish with a fork. Strain liquid off and refrigerate tilapia 10 minutes, or until cool to the touch. Flake into a medium bowl and mix with mayonnaise, mustard, lemon juice, seasoning and onion until all ingredients are incorporated. Stir in shrimp and breadcrumbs. Mixture should be firm enough at this point to form a patty. Gently fold in crabmeat, being careful not to break lumps. Refrigerate 1 hour. Preheat oven to 375°. Scoop out 4 ounces fish mixture and form into a patty. Place on a lightly greased sheet pan. Repeat with remaining mixture. Bake in center of oven 15 to 20 minutes, or until cakes are golden brown. Serve while hot for maximal enjoyment. Yields 6 to 8 cakes.

Restaurant Recipe

Q on Bay

822 Bay Street
Beaufort, SC 29902
843-524-7771
www.qonbay.com • Find us on Facebook

Located on historic Bay Street in downtown Beaufort, Q on Bay is the perfect place to settle down to a wonderful meal with friends and family. This casual restaurant offers indoor dining with a cozy atmosphere and outdoor dining on the largest porch in Beaufort, from which a beautiful view of Beaufort Bay perfectly complements the open-air dining experience. There's nothing quite like happy hour on Q's porch as the sun sets over the Bay. Stop by Q on Bay for live music, authentic Southern barbecue, and home-cooked food that will keep you coming back, time after time.

Monday – Sunday: 11:00 am until

Smoked Chicken Salad

2 pounds smoked chicken, pulled

½ cup small diced red onion

½ cup small diced celery

2 tablespoons bread-and-butter pickle juice

1 tablespoon garlic-salt blend

5 tablespoons mayonnaise

½ teaspoon ground black pepper

In a large mixing bowl, mix all ingredients until well combined. Transfer to a serving bowl and enjoy. Store in a container with a lid. Will keep 3 to 5 days in refrigerator.

Restaurant Recipe

Apple Pancakes

2 cups Bisquick
½ teaspoon cinnamon
1 egg
1⅓ cups milk
¾ cup grated apple

Using an electric mixer, beat baking mix, cinnamon, egg and milk until smooth. Stir in apple. Cook as you normally do pancakes.

Cider Sauce:

1 cup sugar
2 tablespoons cornstarch
½ teaspoon cinnamon
2 cups apple cider
2 tablespoons lemon juice
¼ cup butter

Mix sugar, cornstarch and cinnamon in a saucepan. Stir in cider and lemon juice. Cook over medium high heat, stirring constantly, until mixture boils. Boil 1 minute, stirring constantly, as mixture thickens. Remove from heat and blend in butter. Spoon over pancakes.

Local Favorite

Baked Cheese Balls

½ pound sharp Cheddar cheese, grated
½ stick butter, softened
2 cups Bisquick
6 drops tabasco
¼ teaspoon pepper
½ teaspoon salt
1 teaspoon mustard powder
¼ teaspoon chopped dill

Preheat oven to 375°. In a large bowl, mix cheese and butter until soft. Add Bisquick and seasonings. Moisten with ½ cup water to pie-crust consistency. Roll into walnut-sized balls—makes about 7 dozen. Bake on ungreased cookie sheet for 20 minutes or until lightly brown. These will be slightly puffed and have a flaky texture. They freeze and reheat well. Serve at room temperature. Can make ahead and freeze.

Local Favorite

Butterscotch Brownies

1 stick butter
2 cups light brown sugar
2 eggs
1 cup cake flour
1 teaspoon baking powder
½ teaspoon salt
1 teaspoon vanilla
1 cup chopped pecans
Powdered sugar optional

Preheat oven to 325°. In a mixing bowl, cream butter and sugar; add eggs, one at a time. In another bowl, whisk together flour, baking powder and salt. Add flour mixture to creamed mixture; add vanilla and lastly the nuts. Pour batter into a greased 9x13-inch baking dish. Bake 30 minutes. Cut in squares while still warm and sprinkle with powdered sugar, if desired.

Local Favorite

Barbecued Fish

3 pounds fish
½ teaspoon salt
Dash pepper
1 tablespoon fat or bacon grease
2 tablespoons chopped onions
2 tablespoons vinegar
2 tablespoons brown sugar
3 tablespoons Worcestershire
1 cup ketchup
⅓ cup lemon juice

Preheat oven to 425°. Place fish in a greased shallow baking pan, sprinkle with salt and pepper and set aside. In a skillet over medium-high heat, lightly brown onions in fat; add remaining ingredients, simmering 5 minutes. Pour sauce over fish; bake 35 to 40 minutes, basting fish with sauce every 10 minutes while cooking. Serves 6.

Local Favorite

May River Grill

1263 May River Road, #D
Bluffton, SC 29910
843-757-5755
www.mayrivergrill.com • Find us on Facebook

In 1983, Charlie Sternburgh moved to Hilton Head Island and entered the restaurant business. Guided by his mentor Ed Murray, Charlie learned the ins and outs of the restaurant industry, from serving to managing. He dreamed of opening his own restaurant that would serve truly memorable food featuring fresh ingredients culled from the local rivers and farms. He realized his dream in 2007 with the grand opening of May River Grill. The Grill has earned the accolades of *Wall Street Journal*, *South Carolina Living*, *Taste* magazine, and *Bluffton Today*. Charlie continues today, keeping an eye toward the future and a frying pan to the fire.

Monday – Saturday: 4:45 pm to 9:00 pm

Crispy Flounder with Texas Pete-Brown Butter Sauce

½ cup flour
½ teaspoon kosher salt
½ teaspoon coarse black pepper
½ teaspoon cayenne pepper
3 eggs
1 cup panko breadcrumbs
¼ cup grated Parmesan cheese
1½ pounds flounder fillets
Oil for frying
1 cup brown pot roast gravy
(store bought or homemade)
¼ onion, diced
¼ red bell pepper, diced
¼ green bell pepper, diced
¼ cup Texas Pete hot sauce
1 tablespoon butter

Preheat oven to 350°. In a bowl, mix flour, salt and peppers. In another bowl, whip eggs to make an egg wash. In another bowl, combine breadcrumbs and Parmesan. Dredge fillets in flour mixture, then egg wash; coat both sides evenly with breadcrumb and Parmesan mixture. Fill bottom of a large sauté pan with oil (about ⅛-inch deep) and heat until very hot; brown each side of fillets and transfer to a cookie sheet. Bake 10 minutes. While fish is baking, add gravy, onion, bell peppers and hot sauce to a small sauté pan; bring to a heavy simmer and stir in butter. Plate fillets and top with sauce.

Restaurant Recipe

Sippin Cow

36 Promenade Street
Bluffton, SC 29910
843-757-5051
www.sippincow.com • Find us on Facebook

Welcome to Sippin Cow, a small, cozy café located in the heart of Old Town Bluffton where the charm of small-town life is still alive. Sippin Cow has served fresh, wholesome food in the Bluffton area for more than seventeen years. The menu has remained much the same over the years and has only been enhanced. Guests may dine in, pick up takeout, or book the Café for catering their next special event. The team at Sippin Cow puts a lot of hard work and so much love into pleasing each guest—a service they take much pride in providing. Stop by the Sippin Cow today for a down-home meal made with love.

Tuesday – Saturday: 7:00 am to 3:00 pm
Sunday: 9:00 am to 2:00 pm

Lowcountry Shrimp & Grits

2 tablespoons chicken base
1 cup stone-ground grits
6 tablespoons butter, divided
2 cups shredded sharp Cheddar cheese, divided
1 pound shrimp, peeled and deveined
1 large clove garlic, minced
1 teaspoon Cajun seasoning
1 cup half-and-half
2 tablespoons cornstarch
6 slices bacon, cooked crisp and chopped

In a saucepan over high heat, bring 4 cups water to a boil. Add chicken base. Add grits and cook until water is absorbed, about 20 to 25 minutes. Remove from heat and stir in 3 tablespoons butter and 1½ cups cheese; set aside. Rinse shrimp and pat dry. Melt remaining butter in a large skillet over medium heat. Add garlic and cook until fragrant. Add shrimp, cooking until pink. Add seasoning and sauté shrimp 3 minutes. Add half-and-half and bring to a boil. Meanwhile, make a slurry in a small bowl by mixing cornstarch and 4 tablespoons water until smooth. Add slurry to shrimp mixture and reduce heat to a simmer. Stir continuously until desired thickness is reached. Plate grits and top with shrimp sauce. Garnish with bacon and remaining cheese. Serve immediately. Serves 4.

Restaurant Recipe

Skillet Cornbread

1¼ cups flour
¾ cup yellow cornmeal
2 tablespoons sugar
1 tablespoon baking powder
½ teaspoon salt
½ teaspoon pepper
1 egg
1 cup milk
¼ cup oil
1 (8.75-ounce) can whole kernel corn, drained

Preheat oven to 400°. Coat a 9- or 10-inch cast-iron skillet with cooking spray. Place skillet in oven to heat 5 minutes. In a mixing bowl, whisk together flour, cornmeal, sugar, baking powder, salt and pepper. In another bowl, combine egg, milk and oil. Add liquid ingredients to dry; stir until moistened and combined. Stir in corn. Carefully remove hot skillet from oven and pour in batter. Return to oven and bake 20 to 25 minutes until golden brown. Let cool, cut and enjoy.

Family Favorite

WHERE CAN YOU FIND A PLACE OPEN TO THE PUBLIC SINCE 1870?

Magnolia Plantation is the oldest public tourist site in the Lowcountry and home to the oldest public gardens in America, opening its doors to visitors in 1870. Unlike most of America's gardens, which are formal and seek to control nature, Magnolia cooperates with nature to create a tranquil, Eden-like landscape, where humanity and nature are in harmony.

Founded in 1676 by the Drayton family, Magnolia Plantation has survived the centuries and witnessed the history of our nation unfold—from the American Revolution through the Civil War and beyond.

Thomas Drayton and his wife Ann arrived from Barbados to the new English colony of Charles Towne and established Magnolia Plantation along the Ashley River. They were the first in a direct line of family ownership that has lasted more than 300 years and continues to this day.

In the early 19th century, the gardens at Magnolia truly begin to expand on a grand scale under ownership of John Grimké Drayton. Young John was just 22 years of age when he found himself a wealthy plantation owner after his older brother, Thomas, died on the steps of the plantation of a gunshot wound that was the result of a hunting accident. After entering the Episcopal seminary in New York and marrying Julia Ewing, Thomas returned to Charleston only to contract tuberculosis. His own "cure" for the illness was working outside in the gardens he loved. He also wanted to create a series of romantic gardens for his wife, to make her feel more at home in the South Carolina Lowcountry. A few years later, as though by a miracle, his health returned.

More than anyone else, John Drayton is credited with the informal beauty of the gardens. He introduced the first azaleas to America and was among the first to utilize *Camellia japonica* in an outdoor setting. A great deal of Magnolia's horticultural fame today is based on the large and varied collection of varieties of these two species.

Give fools their gold and knaves their power,
Let fortune's bubbles rise and fall,
Who sows a field or trains a flower
or plants a tree, is more than all.
                                    Whittier

Each subsequent generation of the Drayton family has added their own personal touch to the gardens, expanding and adding to their variety. Today there are various varieties of flowers in bloom, year-round, from camellias, daffodils, and azaleas to countless other species, with a climax of incredible beauty at the arrival of the spring bloom.

You can step back in time with a guided tour of the Drayton family home, the core of which was built prior to the Revolutionary War, near Summerville, and floated down the Ashley River to Magnolia after the Civil War; take a tram tour of the plantation's wetlands, lakes, forests, and marshes; enjoy the Rice Field Boat Tour through Magnolia's old, flooded rice field along the Ashley River; or visit the Zoo & Nature Center to interact with a variety of animals native to the area that are more than happy to be met, pet, and fed. All this and more await you at Charleston's first tourist destination.

Magnolia Plantation and Gardens

**3550 Ashley River Road
Charleston, SC 29414
843-571-1266
www.magnoliaplantation.com**

The Mason Jar by Fatboys

2487 Ashley River Road, Suite 4
Charleston, SC 29414
843-203-3290
Find us on Facebook

The Mason Jar by Fatboys offers a range of fresh dishes bursting with flavor. Serving the Charleston area since 2014, this homey restaurant provides great tasting food prepared fresh from the highest quality ingredients. Treat yourself today with a delicious, traditional Lowcountry meal from the extensive menu. Come in for pulled pork, local seafood and veggies, handmade burgers, fried chicken, and so much more. You are sure to enjoy the down-home atmosphere, friendly service, and affordable prices. The Mason Jar by Fatboys is proudly preserving Lowcountry tradition.

Wednesday – Friday: 11:00 am to 9:00 pm
Saturday: 8:00 am to 9:00 pm
Sunday: 8:30 am to 3:00 pm

PRESERVING
LOWCOUNTRY
TRADITION

Pimento Cheese Dip

1 (8-ounce) package cream
cheese, softened
6 cups shredded Cheddar cheese
1½ cups mayonnaise
1 teaspoon onion powder
1 teaspoon garlic powder
¼ teaspoon paprika
1 teaspoon salt
1 teaspoon pepper
½ cup smashed pimentos

In a large bowl, beat cream cheese until smooth. Add remaining ingredients and mix well. Refrigerate before serving. Pairs well with pork skins or crackers. Dip can also be used as a spread on a variety of sandwiches.

Restaurant Recipe

BLT Dip

1 pound bacon
1 cup mayonnaise
1 cup sour cream
1 tomato, peeled, seeded and diced

Cook bacon in a large deep skillet over medium high heat until evenly browned; drain on paper towels. In a medium bowl, combine mayonnaise with sour cream; crumble in bacon. Mix in tomatoes just before serving.

Local Favorite

Boiled Peanuts

2 pounds raw green peanuts in the shell
1 cup plain salt

Wash peanuts to remove any dust or dirt. Fill a large stockpot 3 quarters full of water; add peanuts and salt. Place on stove over medium-high heat and bring to a rolling boil. Place lid on pot, reduce heat to medium and boil 3 hours. Make sure water completely covers peanuts at all times. Cut off heat and let sit for 30 minutes. Taste to make sure peanuts are to the desired doneness. Serve warm and enjoy.

Note: For Cajun peanuts, cut salt to ½ cup and add 1 cup Cajun seasoning.

Local Favorite

Bicycle Wreck

3 tablespoons olive oil
1 medium onion, chopped
1 green bell pepper chopped
1 medium carrot, sliced
2 medium zucchinis, sliced
1½ cups bulgur wheat
1 (14-ounce) can stewed tomatoes
1 teaspoon paprika
⅛ teaspoon cayenne pepper
½ teaspoon salt
1 pound tofu, cubed

In a skillet over medium-high heat, sauté vegetables in oil for 3 minutes. Add bulgar; cook until it crackles. Add tomatoes, ½ cup water and seasonings. Place lid on skillet, reduce heat to low and cook 25 minutes. Add more water, if necessary. Stir in tofu just before serving.

Local Favorite

Crab Melts

½ pound white crabmeat,
fresh or canned
1 tablespoon chopped celery
1 teaspoon Dijon mustard
2 tablespoons red pepper
Salt and pepper to taste
2 tablespoons sour cream
4 slices Monterey Jack cheese
1 (4- to 5-inch) baguette sliced

In a mixing bowl, combine ingredients.
Slice baguette in half lengthwise. Spread
crabmeat mixture evenly over each half.
Place under broiler until melted.

Local Favorite

Fresh Peach Milkshake

3 medium-size peaches,
peeled and sliced
4 cups vanilla ice cream
1 cup milk
1 teaspoon vanilla extract

Combine all ingredients in a blender.
Blend until smooth. Serve and enjoy.

Local Favorite

Crabby Carolina Rice

1½ cups Carolina long-grain white rice
1 tablespoon Old Bay Seasoning
2½ tablespoons unsalted butter
14 ounces crabmeat
1 tablespoon oil
1 medium onion, finely chopped
2 garlic cloves, minced
½ cup chopped canned
tomatoes, drained
1 teaspoon fresh lemon juice
Salt
2 scallions, thinly slices

In a large saucepan over high heat, bring
4 cups water to a boil; add rice and cook
12 minutes stirring occasionally. Drain
and spread on baking sheet to cool. In
a large skillet, toast Old Bay Seasoning
over low heat 40 seconds. Scrape into a
small bowl: set aside to cool. Melt butter
in skillet over medium-high heat. Add
crabmeat and 1 teaspoon toasted Old
Bay Seasoning. Cooking 1½ minutes,
tossing gently with a spatula. Transfer
crabmeat to plate. Heat oil in skillet, add
onion; cook over low heat until softened.
Add garlic and remaining toasted Old
Bay; cook 2 minutes. Add tomatoes and
cook 4 minutes or until dry. Add rice
and cook over moderate heat 3 minutes
or until heated through. Add crabmeat
and lemon juice; cook until hot, while
stirring. Season with salt and transfer to
warmed bowls. Garnish with scallions
over rice and serve.

Local Favorite

MOE'S
CROSSTOWN TAVERN
714 Rutledge Ave.
641-0469

714 Rutledge Avenue
Charleston, SC 29403
843-641-0469
www.moescrosstowntavern.com
Find us on Facebook

Opened in 1998, Moe's Crosstown Tavern is a vintage pub located in downtown Charleston near Hampton Park. Moe's is the local destination for excellent food, great drinks, and a welcoming atmosphere. Catch a ballgame on one of the big screen TVs, rack up a game of pool with a few friends, or spend your time eating your way through the amazing menu. Moe's goes above and beyond to offer you a superior selection of drinks, whether you prefer an ice-cold beer or a stiff drink. Stop by today and have a delicious burger and a tasty craft beer while you kick back and forget your troubles.

Monday – Saturday: 11:00 am to 2:00 am
Sunday: 10:30 am to 2:00 am

Rutledge Burger

Fried Tomato Slices:

2 cups panko breadcrumbs
1 tablespoon dried oregano
1 teaspoon granulated garlic
1 large beefsteak tomato, thickly sliced
Cornstarch as needed
Buttermilk as needed

Preheat deep fryer to 350°. In a bowl, mix together breadcrumbs, oregano and garlic. Coat tomato slices in cornstarch, dip in buttermilk and toss in breadcrumb mixture. Fry until golden brown and drain on paper towels.

2 pounds ground beef, divided
into 4 patties
4 brioche buns
8 slices thick-cut bacon, fried crisp
8 tablespoons Moe's Pimento Cheese
4 Fried Tomato Slices
Spring mix greens to taste

Grill burgers to desired doneness. To assemble, place patties on bottom buns. Top each patty with 2 tablespoons Pimento Cheese (next page), 2 slices bacon, 1 tomato slice, spring mix greens and top bun.

Restaurant Recipe

Pimento Cheese

2 cups shredded sharp Cheddar cheese

⅔ cup shredded Parmesan cheese

2 ounces cream cheese, softened

½ cup mayonnaise

¼ cup jalapeño, seeded and diced

1 (6-ounce) jar roasted red peppers, diced (plus juice)

2 tablespoons finely diced curly parsley

Blend all ingredients together in a mixer on medium speed. Refrigerate at least 2 hours.

Restaurant Recipe

Bacon Pancakes with Pecan–Bourbon Caramel Sauce

1½ cups all-purpose flour

4 teaspoons baking powder

1 teaspoon salt

1 tablespoon sugar

1¼ cups milk

1 egg

3 tablespoons melted butter

1 tablespoon vanilla extract

6 slices bacon, chopped, cooked and drained

Powdered sugar and whipped cream, optional

Pecan–Bourbon Caramel Sauce:

3 cups sugar

¾ pound butter, divided

1½ cups heavy cream

1 (8-ounce) bag chopped pecans

1½ ounces bourbon or to taste

Sift flour, baking powder, salt and sugar into a large bowl. Mix in milk, egg, butter and vanilla; set aside. To make Pecan-Bourbon Caramel Sauce, add sugar and 1½ cups water to a large pot over medium heat; stir until sugar is dissolved. Heat until mixture starts to caramelize. Remove from heat and stir in ½ pound butter and heavy cream. Melt remaining butter in a saucepan over medium heat; add pecans and bourbon, cooking until pecans are toasted. Stir pecans into caramelized mixture. On a greased griddle set on medium-high heat, place ¼ cup batter; sprinkle with bacon. Flip pancakes when bubbles appear on top and cook until other side is browned. Plate and top with Pecan-Bourbon Caramel Sauce. Powdered sugar and whipped cream are optional.

Restaurant Recipe

60 Bull Café

**60 Bull Street
Charleston, SC 29401
843-718-3145
www.60bull.com**

Your Local Café for Breakfast, Lunch & Supper

Nestled among historic oaks and stately Charleston residences, 60 Bull Café enlivens Harleston Village with bright, interesting offerings and approachable, relaxed seating. At 60 Bull Café, many neighborhood streets, homes, and trees look just like they did hundreds of years ago. Guests will enjoy friendly service, takeaway wine and beer selections, fresh-made food, great standbys, and new local favorites in regular rotation on the menu. Stroll into the Café for a bite, or linger into the evening over a glass of wine on the patio. Visit soon and often.

**Tuesday – Saturday: 9:00 am to 9:00 pm
Sunday: 9:00 am to 3:00 pm**

Shrimp & Grits

1 tablespoon olive oil

1 pound Lowcountry brown shrimp (or Gulf white shrimp), peeled and deveined

2 Roma tomatoes, small diced

1 teaspoon kosher salt

1 teaspoon black pepper

4 slices bacon, cooked crisp and diced

1 cup shrimp stock

1 tablespoon butter

2 small green onions, diced

4 to 6 cups prepared grits

In a large skillet over medium heat, warm olive oil. Add shrimp; sauté 1 minute. Add tomatoes, salt and pepper; sauté 1 minute. Add bacon; sauté 1 minute. Add stock, butter and green onion. Reduce 2 minutes, stirring constantly, while butter incorporates. Divide evenly over 4 to 6 bowls of grits. Enjoy.

Executive Chef Joel Vetsch
Restaurant Recipe

Café Cobblers

4 cups fresh fruit (peeled apples, peeled peaches, berries, etc.)

2 tablespoons sugar

1 teaspoon cinnamon

1 teaspoon salt

2 cups self-rising flour

2 cups packed brown sugar

1½ cups half-and-half (or heavy cream)

Granola for topping

Vanilla ice cream

Preheat oven to 350° and grease 2 glass pie dishes. In a mixing bowl, stir together fruit, sugar, cinnamon and salt. Fill each prepared pie dishes to top with fruit mixture. In a mixing bowl, whisk together flour and brown sugar; slowly whisk in half-and-half. Pour half of flour mixture evenly over tops of each cobbler. Bake 55 minutes. Sprinkle tops with granola and let rest 15 minutes. Serve with ice cream. Makes 2 cobblers.

Executive Chef Joel Vetsch
Restaurant Recipe

Sunflower Café

2366 Ashley River Road
Charleston, SC 29414
843-571-1773
www.sunflowercafecharleston.com • Find us on Facebook

Sunflower Café opened in August 2005. This local, family-owned restaurant serves breakfast and lunch. The restaurant's day-to-day operations are overseen by a team that spans three generations. Owner Jenny Hooker and Executive Chef Jennifer Adams, her daughter, are joined by Jenny's granddaughter, Rhiannon Passarini. Guests may also meet family matriarch Betty Jean "MaMa" Huggins, who knows many of the local regulars. The Café's Sweet Potato Pancakes with Toasted Pecan Butter recipe was even featured in an episode of Rachel Ray's *$40 a Day*. The Fried Green Tomato and Crab Benedict was voted #16 out of 50 best Benedicts in the U.S. by Four Square. Stop by today for a Southern-style meal in a wholesome setting.

Tuesday – Saturday: 8:00 am to 2:00 pm
Sunday: 9:00 am to 2:00 pm

Best Sandwich in Charleston

Red Onion Aioli:

2 cloves garlic
Pinch salt
1 large egg yolk
2 teaspoons fresh lemon juice
½ teaspoon Dijon mustard
¼ cup extra-virgin olive oil
3 tablespoons vegetable oil
**1 large red onion, chopped
and caramelized**
Salt and pepper to taste

On a flat surface, mash garlic and salt to a paste with a large knife. Whisk together yolk, lemon juice, and mustard in a bowl. Combine oils in a measuring cup; add a few drops at a time to yolk mixture, whisking constantly until all oil is incorporated. Whisk in garlic paste, onion, salt and pepper. Chill until ready to use.

Sandwich:

4 focaccia buns
4 (4-ounce) petite fillet mignons, grilled
1 cup shredded baby Swiss cheese

Slice focaccia buns in half. Spread Red Onion Aioli over insides of top and bottom. Top a bottom slice with a fillet mignon. Top with ¼ cup cheese. Repeat for 3 more sandwiches. Optional: serve with au jus for dipping.

Restaurant Recipe

Sweet Potato Pancakes with Toasted Pecan Butter

Toasted Pecan Butter:

**¼ cup finely chopped pecans,
toasted and cooled**
½ pound butter, softened
½ teaspoon cinnamon
1 teaspoon vanilla extract
1 tablespoon brown sugar
1 tablespoon honey

Mix all ingredients together in a bowl. Roll up into a cylinder in parchment paper; freeze. Cut into slices.

Pancakes:

1 cup all-purpose flour
1 cup whole-wheat flour
4 teaspoons baking powder
2 tablespoons brown sugar
1 teaspoon cinnamon
Pinch nutmeg
2 cups milk
2 eggs
**1 sweet potato, cooked until tender,
peeled and puréed**
**4 teaspoons melted butter, plus more for
greasing skillet**

In a large bowl, combine all ingredients. Whisk together until smooth. Cook batches in a buttered skillet over medium-high heat until bubbles form on surface; flip and cook until dark golden brown. Serve with Toasted Pecan Butter and maple syrup. Makes 10 servings.

Restaurant Recipe

Skillets Café & Grill

1 North Forest Beach Drive, Unit J
Hilton Head Island, SC 29928
843-785-3131
skilletscafe.com • Facebook.com/skilletscafeandgrill

Now celebrating twenty-five years, Skillets Café & Grill prepares delicious, home-style Southern and seafood dishes. Enjoy classic and creative breakfasts; sandwiches and endless salad bar; and favorites like shrimp and grits, Lowcountry boil, jambalaya, seafood platters, crab cakes, pork chops, ribs, steak, fried chicken, pasta dishes, okra, collard greens, fried green tomatoes, and more. There are healthy and gluten-free options, daily specials, kids menus, takeout, and catering. Dine indoors or out on pet-friendly patios, one street over from the beach.

Breakfast & Lunch:
Daily: 7:00 am to 4:00 pm
Dinner:
Daily: 4:00 pm to 10:00 pm in season

Skillets' Stuffed French Toast

12 large eggs

1 quart half-and-half

¾ cup vanilla extract

¼ teaspoon salt

1½ tablespoon cinnamon

½ tablespoon nutmeg

¾ cup sugar

30 slices Texas toast

3 (18-ounce) jars apricot preserves

2 (8-ounce) packages cream
cheese, softened

In a large bowl, combine eggs, half-and-half and vanilla. In another bowl, combine salt, cinnamon, nutmeg and sugar. Add dry ingredients to wet ingredients; mix well. Dip Texas toast into batter and set on a sheet pan. In a nonstick skillet over medium heat, cook toast until golden brown on each side, flipping once. In another bowl, combine preserves and cream cheese; cut a slit in each toast slice and stuff with apricot filling.

Restaurant Recipe

Shrimp & Grits

1 white onion, small diced and sautéed

3 red bell peppers, small
diced and sautéed

½ pound smoked sausage,
sliced and cooked

¾ cup diced cooked bacon

1½ quarts half-and-half

2 quarts heavy cream

1 cup chicken broth

1 tablespoon hot sauce

Salt and pepper to taste

½ cup cornstarch

3 cups grits, prepared according to
package directions

Cooked shrimp, amount and size
according to preference

Add all ingredients except cornstarch, grits and shrimp to a saucepan over medium heat; bring to a boil. Add cornstarch and stir until sauce thickens; remove from heat. To serve, ladle grits into a bowl and top with sauce. Add shrimp. Makes 10 to 12 servings.

Restaurant Recipe

Skull Creek Boathouse

397 Squire Pope Road
Hilton Head Island, SC 29926
843-681-3663
www.skullcreekboathouse.com • Find us on Facebook

Skull Creek Boathouse is Hilton Head Island's most awarded landmark waterfront restaurant. Located on the scenic banks of Skull Creek, just inland from the South Carolina coast, you'll enjoy beautiful views, fresh local seafood, unique sushi creations, and some of the best cocktails around. Try the Seafood Extravaganza, a feast of snow crab legs, mussels, clams, and oysters that Executive Chef Brad Blake describes as the "epitome of the Skull Creek Boathouse." Visit Skull Creek Boathouse to experience tasty dishes, beautiful sunsets, and what some call the "Boathouse State of Mind."

Monday – Friday: 11:00 am to 10:00 pm
Saturday & Sunday: 10:00 am to 10:00 pm

Flounder Melt

This recipe is universal for most local South Carolina fish. The most important part is to find the freshest fish available. We like to use flounder.

2 tablespoons butter, divided
1 slice rye bread
1 yellow onion, julienned
1 pound mushrooms, sliced
1 cup mayonnaise
½ teaspoon minced garlic
½ teaspoon lemon juice
1 teaspoon Old Bay seasoning
1 cup paprika
2 tablespoons cayenne pepper
2 tablespoons black pepper
2 tablespoons white pepper
2 tablespoons dried thyme
¼ cup salt
1 skin-on flounder fillet
Slice Swiss cheese to taste

Spread 1 tablespoon butter over bread and grill; set aside. In a large skillet over low heat, sauté onion and mushrooms in remaining butter 5 to 7 minutes, or until caramelized; set aside. In a bowl, blend together mayonnaise, garlic, lemon juice and Old Bay seasoning to make Old Bay aioli sauce; set aside. Preheat a cast-iron skillet over high heat. In another bowl, toss together paprika, cayenne pepper, black pepper, white pepper, dried thyme and salt to make blackening spice. Dredge flounder in blackening spice. Place flounder flesh side down in preheated skillet; flip after 2 minutes. Top with Swiss cheese and let melt. Remove flounder from skillet and place on rye; top with mushrooms and onions. Finish with a drizzle of aioli and serve.

Restaurant Recipe

Fresh Cherry Cake

12 ounces fresh black cherries, pitted
½ stick butter, softened
1 cup sugar
2 eggs, room temperature
1 cup buttermilk
1 teaspoon vanilla
1½ cups self-rising flour
½ cup white cornmeal
½ teaspoon almond extract
¼ cup powdered sugar

Preheat oven to 350°. Butter a 9-inch spring form pan and line bottom with parchment paper. Slice half the black cherries; leave the rest whole. In the bowl of a stand mixer using the paddle attachment, beat together butter and sugar for 3 minutes. Add eggs, one at a time, beating after each on low speed until mixed and light in color. Add buttermilk and vanilla; mix until all is combined. In a small bowl, mix together flour and cornmeal. Using a large spatula, fold flour mixture into wet ingredients until incorporated. Do not overmix. Add sliced cherries and almond extract to the empty bowl and toss to combine. Pour half the batter into prepared pan. Arrange sliced cherries on top, then pour remaining batter over cherries. Smooth batter to the edge of the pan. Arrange whole cherries across the top of the cake batter, slightly pushing down. Bake 45 to 50 minutes or until a skewer inserted into the center comes out clean. Remove cake from oven and rest on a cooking rack 15 to 20 minutes before removing outside ring. Remove ring and rest until cool enough to remove parchment paper and place on a cake plate. Dust with a light sprinkle of powdered sugar.

Local Favorite

Potato-Onion Fans

1 medium baking potato
1 medium shallot, sliced
Salt and pepper to taste
1 tablespoon butter
1 tablespoon sour cream
1 teaspoon chopped chives

Preheat oven to 400°. Scrub potato, but do not peel. Place potato on cutting board and cut ¼-inch slices without cutting all the way through—just enough to make potato fan out. Place a slice of shallot between each potato slice carefully so you do not break the potato. Sprinkle potato with salt and pepper and dot with butter on each cut. Loosely wrap in heavy-duty foil. Bake 1 hour or until done. Open the foil carefully to release steam. Top with sour cream and chives, and serve immediately.

Local Favorite

Zesty Cheezy Cauliflower

1 medium head cauliflower
¼ cup sour cream
¼ cup mayonnaise
2 teaspoons spicy mustard
1 cup shredded Cheddar cheese

Break cauliflower into flowerettes. Place in a 2-quart round casserole dish. Add 2 tablespoons water and cover. Microwave on high 6 to 8 minutes or until almost tender; drain. Mix sour cream, mayonnaise and mustard. Toss gently with cauliflower. Sprinkle with cheese. Microwave on medium 2 to 4 minutes. Serves 4 to 6.

Local Favorite

Skull Creek Dockside

2 Hudson Road
Hilton Head Island, SC 29926
843-785-3625
www.docksidehhi.com
Find us on Facebook

Skull Creek Dockside restaurant dropped anchor in November 2017, forever changing the culinary landscape of the Lowcountry. The restaurant resembles an old-style river house with authentic architecture, reclaimed wood, and nautical accents reminiscent of a Melville novel. Full-pane glass windows showcase the sweeping waterfront view, which can also be enjoyed from the covered dining patio and Sharkbar. Guests will enjoy a menu combining popular American and Southern staples, including delicious steaks, barbecue, and seafood. The space also houses a stage for live music, an adult space with games, and the Shrimp Boat playground for kids.

Sunday – Thursday: 11:00 am to 10:00 pm
Friday & Saturday: 11:00 am to 11:00 pm

Shrimp & Grits with BBQ Drizzle

2 sticks butter, divided

6 cups chicken stock, divided

2 cups Anson Mills grits

¼ cup salt plus more for seasoning

2 tablespoons black pepper plus more for seasoning

1 each green, red and yellow bell pepper, ¼-inch dice

1 yellow onion, ¼-inch diced

2 tablespoons chopped garlic

2 tablespoons plus 1 teaspoon dried thyme

1 cup tomato juice

1 cup paprika

2 tablespoons cayenne pepper

2 tablespoons white pepper

¼ cup brown sugar

2 pounds fresh (16/20) white shrimp, peeled and deveined

1 pound andouille sausage, sliced

In a large pot over high heat, melt 1 stick butter and add 4 cups stock; bring to boil. Add grits, stirring constantly. Reduce heat, continuing to stir. Slowly add remaining stock and butter as needed. Cook 45 minutes, or until grits are done. Add salt and pepper to taste; set aside. In a large saucepan over low heat, add bell peppers, onion, garlic, 1 teaspoon thyme and tomato juice; simmer 8 to 10 minutes and set aside. In a bowl, prepare BBQ spice by tossing together the ¼ cup salt, 2 tablespoons black pepper, 2 tablespoons dried thyme, paprika, cayenne, white pepper and brown sugar; toss shrimp in spice to coat. In a skillet over medium heat, sear shrimp with sausage 3 to 4 minutes, or until shrimp are cooked through; remove from heat. Ladle grits into center of plate and fan shrimp around edge with tails facing out. Spoon sausage, peppers and onions into center.

BBQ Drizzle:

1¼ cups tomato paste

1¼ cups ketchup

2¼ cups brown sugar

½ cup dark molasses

½ cup apple cider vinegar

½ cup water

1 tablespoon Worcestershire sauce

5 teaspoons dry mustard

1 teaspoons granulated garlic

4 teaspoons paprika

½ teaspoons cayenne pepper

2 teaspoons black pepper

3 teaspoons kosher salt

Mix together all ingredients in a bowl until well combined. Drizzle over top of warm Shrimp & Grits. Enjoy.

Restaurant Recipe

Sea Biscuit Café

21 JC Long Boulevard
Isle of Palms, SC 29451
843-886-4079
Find us on Facebook

Sea Biscuit Café began in 1985, remodeled from a small beach cottage used as a repair shop. Opened January 1986, it quickly became obvious the Café needed more space, and a large screened porch was added. After three successful years, Hurricane Hugo removed its roof and forced yet another remodel. Hugo changed the flavor of the island, prompting construction of rental homes and making the Café part of the "old" Isle of Palms. Continuing in tradition, Sea Biscuit Café still serves its original menu with a few new additions. Visit for classic café fare like soups, salads, sandwiches, and delicious early morning breakfasts.

Monday – Friday: 6:30 am to 2:30 pm
Saturday & Sunday: 7:30 am to 1:00 pm

Spinach, Tomato & Feta Quiche

3 cups chopped fresh spinach
1 cup chopped tomato
1 cup crumbled feta
1 (9-inch) deep-dish pie shell,
    partially prebaked
4 eggs
1 cup half-and-half
¼ teaspoon nutmeg
Salt and pepper to taste

Preheat oven to 350°. Layer spinach, tomato and feta into pie shell. In a bowl, beat together eggs, half-and-half, nutmeg, salt and pepper; pour into pie shell. Bake 30 to 40 minutes, or until puffy and light brown.

Restaurant Recipe

Banana Bread

1 cup mashed bananas
2 eggs
½ cup canola oil
1 cup sugar
1 teaspoon vanilla extract
2 cups all-purpose flour
1 teaspoon baking soda
½ teaspoon salt

Preheat oven to 350°. In a large bowl, beat together bananas, eggs, oil, sugar and vanilla. In another bowl, sift together flour, baking soda and salt; stir into banana mixture just until combined. Pour into a greased 5x9-inch loaf pan. Bake 50 to 60 minutes, or until a toothpick inserted into center comes out clean.

Restaurant Recipe

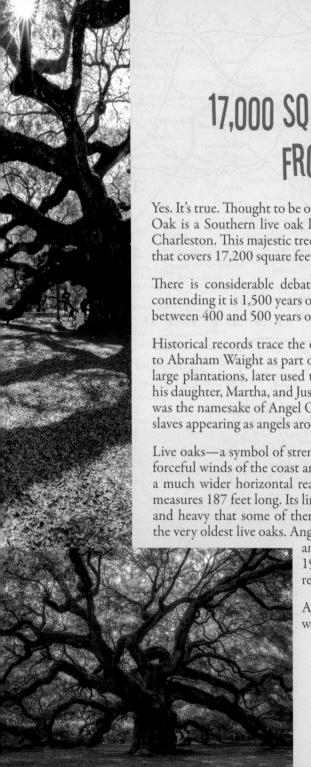

17,000 SQUARE FEET OF SHADE FROM ONE TREE?

Yes. It's true. Thought to be one of the oldest living things in the country, Angel Oak is a Southern live oak located in Angel Oak Park, on Johns Island near Charleston. This majestic tree stands more than 65 feet tall and produces shade that covers 17,200 square feet.

There is considerable debate about the age of the Angel Oak, with some contending it is 1,500 years old. Most believe the more conservative estimate of between 400 and 500 years old.

Historical records trace the ownership of the tree to 1717, when it was given to Abraham Waight as part of a land grant. Waight, a wealthy owner of several large plantations, later used the land as part of a marriage settlement between his daughter, Martha, and Justus Angel. Their estate was called Angel Estate and was the namesake of Angel Oak. Local folklore tells stories of ghosts of former slaves appearing as angels around the tree.

Live oaks—a symbol of strength in the South—have evolved to withstand the forceful winds of the coast and are, therefore, shorter than other trees but have a much wider horizontal reach. From tip to tip, Angel Oak's longest branch measures 187 feet long. Its limbs, the size of tree trunks themselves, are so large and heavy that some of them rest on the ground, a feature common to only the very oldest live oaks. Angel Oak has survived countless earthquakes, floods, and hurricanes, including Hurricane Hugo in 1989, when it was severely damaged but ultimately recovered and continued to grow.

Angel Oak is a beautifully majestic site, not be missed when traveling the South Carolina Lowcountry.

Fun Facts about Live Oaks

▼ They are called "live oaks" because the trees remain green and "alive" throughout the winter, when other oak trees are dormant and leafless.

▼ A mature live oak tree can draw up to fifty gallons of water per day through its tap root deep in the ground.

▼ Large, sprawling, picturesque trees, live oaks are usually graced with Spanish moss and are strongly reminiscent of the Old South.

Angel Oak Park

**3688 Angel Oak Road
Johns Island, SC 29455**

**Charleston City Parks:
843-724-7324**

ANGEL OAK
•RESTAURANT•

3669 Savannah Highway
Johns Island, SC 29449
843-556-7525
www.angeloakrestaurant.com • Find us on Facebook

Welcome to Angel Oak Restaurant, a charming eatery serving up Southern-style American food. The Angel Oak approach is simple: obtain the freshest ingredients in season and present them in a way that best represents the area. Much of the menu changes with the seasons. Guests will enjoy a lunch menu that provides fresh, rustic, scratch-made food and a dinner menu that emphasizes innovative approaches to Southern classics, each complete with specialty beer or wine. Stop in to share a few appetizers over of a bottle of wine, enjoy a country-fried steak with local beer, or explore one of the alluring entrées. Don't forget to save room for dessert.

Tuesday – Saturday: 11:00 am until
Sunday: 10:00 am to 3:00 pm

Pimento Cheese

5 cups shredded Cheddar cheese
½ pound mascarpone
2 cups mayonnaise
2 cups chopped roasted red peppers
4 dashes Tabasco sauce
1 teaspoon cayenne pepper
2 teaspoons salt

Mix all ingredients together in a large bowl. Purée in processor until semi-smooth.

Restaurant Recipe

Pimento Cheese Grits

3 quarts chicken stock
1 cup milk
1 stick butter
4 cups stone-ground grits
1 cup Pimento Cheese
Salt and pepper to taste

Combine stock, milk and butter in a stockpot over low heat and bring to simmer. Using a wooden spoon, stir in grits. Simmer about 40 minutes, stirring every 2 minutes to prevent sticking. Add Pimento Cheese. Adjust seasoning with salt and pepper.

Restaurant Recipe

Boone Hall Farms Market Café

2521 Highway 17 North
Mount Pleasant, SC 29466
843-856-8154
www.boonehallfarms.com

Boone Hall Farms Market Café is one of the Charleston area's hidden gems. Sample delicious smoked chicken, barbecue ribs, pulled pork, or brisket, all cooked up by Mr. Tom on a custom-made smoker. Add collards and Miss Suzanne's Tomato Pie, and man, oh man, you've got a combination so good it could "make a puppy pull a freight train up a dirt road." The diverse menu also includes farm-fresh meals, salads, sandwiches, wraps, various sides, and homemade desserts that are as good as grandma makes. The Café is located inside Boone Hall Farms Market, a venue that's part farmers market, part specialty store. Drop by and check out this one-of-a-kind destination.

Boone Hall Farms Market:
Monday – Saturday: 9:00 am to 7:00 pm
Sunday: 10:00 am to 6:00 pm
Market Café:
Monday – Saturday: 11:00 am to 6:00 pm
Sunday: 11:00 am to 5:00 pm

(Expanded hours for both the Market and the Café
during the summer season)

Boone Hall Farms Collard Greens

10 slices Applewood smoked bacon, diced

1 large sweet onion, julienned

2 bunches Boone Hall Farms collards, stemmed, chopped and rinsed

1 smoked ham hock

2 cups cider vinegar

3 tablespoons ham base

¼ cup Tabasco sauce

2 teaspoons black pepper

1½ cups sugar

Cook bacon in large stockpot over medium heat until crispy. Add onion and cook 5 to 8 minutes or until tender. Add remaining ingredients plus 3 quarts water. Set heat to high and bring to a boil; reduce heat to a simmer. Cover and simmer 2 to 3 hours or until collards are tender. Adjust seasoning to taste.

Restaurant Recipe

Miss Suzanne's Tomato Pie

1½ cups shredded Cheddar cheese

¾ cup shredded mozzarella

2 green onions, chopped

Fresh basil to taste, chopped

1 cup mayonnaise

Salt and pepper to taste

4 tomatoes, sliced

1 (9-inch) pie shell, precooked

Preheat oven to 350°. In a large bowl, combine all ingredients except tomatoes and pie shell to make cheese mix; set aside. Evenly layer tomatoes in bottom of pie shell. Top with cheese mix. Bake 15 minutes or until cheese is lightly browned on top.

Restaurant Recipe

Jack's Cosmic Dogs

2805 Highway 17 North
Mount Pleasant, SC 29466
843-884-7677
www.jackscosmicdogs.com • Find us on Facebook

Remember your youth when you washed your car and drove to your favorite hot dog stand for long-neck sodas, soft-serve ice cream, amazing hot dogs, and fresh-cut fries? Jack Hurley and family opened Jack's Cosmic Dogs in the late 90's. Reminiscent of roadside hot dog stands from Jack's youth, Jack's serves cosmic dogs, vegetarian options, meatloaf, and chicken sandwiches. Known for its Sweet Potato Mustard, Blue Cheese Coleslaw, and quirky atmosphere, Jack's has been on the Food Network and voted Best Hot Dog in Charleston since 2000. Alton Brown calls Jack's dogs "the best hot dog" he's ever had. Bring your family and friends to Jack's Cosmic Dogs, and travel back to your future.

Daily: 10:30 am to 8:00 pm

Jack's Blue Cheese Coleslaw

Blue Cheese Dressing:

1 cup crumbled blue cheese
1 cup mayonnaise
1 cup sour cream
2 tablespoons apple cider vinegar
1 teaspoon honey (or sugar)
2 teaspoons Worcestershire sauce
Salt, pepper or other seasonings to taste

In a large bowl, combine all ingredients. Mix until well combined. Makes 10 servings.

Slaw:

1 small green cabbage, shredded
1 small red cabbage, shredded

In a large bowl, combine two-thirds green cabbage to one-third red cabbage. Add Blue Cheese Dressing to taste and toss to combine.

Restaurant Recipe

Pan-Fried Sea Scallops with Lemon Butter

¼ cup flour
½ teaspoon salt
¼ teaspoon pepper
8 to 10 ounces sea scallops
4 tablespoons butter, divided
2 teaspoons lemon juice
2 teaspoons chopped parsley
4 lemon wedges

In a bowl, combine flour, salt and pepper. Dredge scallops in flour mixture; shake off excess. In a large heavy skillet over medium-high heat, melt 2 tablespoons butter. Add scallops and cook about 3 to 4 minutes, turning occasionally, until golden brown outside and opaque inside; remove from pan and plate. Reduce heat to low and add remaining butter, stirring up browned bits until butter melts. Whisk in lemon juice and parsley. Spoon over scallops and garnish with lemon wedges.

Local Favorite

Garlic Cheese Bread

3 tablespoons olive oil
2 tablespoons butter, softened
2 garlic cloves, minced
1 (1-pound) loaf French bread,
split lengthwise
3 tablespoons grated Parmesan cheese
Paprika to taste

Preheat broiler. In a small bowl, combine oil, butter and garlic; mix well. Place bread on a baking sheet, spread garlic butter evenly on cut sides, sprinkle evenly with cheese and dust with paprika. Place in broiler 5 inches under heat. Cook 1 to 2 minutes, or until cheese is bubbly and flecked with brown. Cut into slices and serve.

Local Favorite

Spicy Pot Roast

1 (4-pound) chuck (or rump) roast
2 tablespoons oil
1 (16-ounce) can diced tomatoes
3 teaspoons salt
1½ teaspoons black pepper
2 teaspoons chili powder
¼ teaspoon red pepper
1 large onion, sliced
2 bay leaves
1 teaspoon thyme
¼ cup wine (or sherry), optional
Parsley, chopped

In a Dutch oven over medium-high heat, brown roast in oil. Add 2 cups water and remaining ingredients except parsley; simmer 2½ hours, covered. Slice roast; plate and cover with sauce; top with parsley and enjoy. This roast is always better the second day and freezes well for later use.

Local Favorite

Chicken Stew

6 bone-in chicken breasts
1 cup chopped tomatoes
1 (6-ounce) can tomato paste
1 (14.75-ounce) can cream-style corn
1 small potato, diced
½ onion, diced
½ (16-ounce) package spaghetti, cooked
1 tablespoon butter
Salt and pepper to taste

In a large saucepan over high heat, boil chicken until tender; debone and shred, reserving broth. Add tomatoes, paste, corn, potato, onion and spaghetti to reserved broth. Season to taste with butter, salt and pepper. Cook slowly until all vegetables are done. Stir in chicken. Serves 8.

Local Favorite

On Forty-One

1055 Highway 41
Mount Pleasant, SC 29466
843-352-9235
www.onfortyone.com • Find us on Facebook at On Forty One

Chef Brannon and Renee Florie opened On Forty-One in November 2014. Both seasoned restaurateurs, they wanted diners to enjoy classic Southern cooking in a relaxed, comfortable setting. Chef's long-lasting relationships with local South Carolina farmers and purveyors allows for diners to experience truly local, farm-fresh cuisine. The menu features everything from fried chicken to smoked pork chops and more. Open Tuesday through Sunday for happy hour, dinner, and Sunday brunch. Stop by, come in, and enjoy the freshest taste of the Lowcountry.

Tuesday – Saturday: 4:00 pm to 10:00 pm
Sunday: 10:00 am to 2:00 pm

Collard Greens

Collards are a staple at On Forty-One.

2 cups julienned Vidalia onions
½ cup cider vinegar
½ cup red wine vinegar
2 sticks butter
2 quarts chicken stock
8 dashes hot sauce
1 smoked ham hock
Salt and pepper to taste
5 pounds collards, cleaned and chopped

Add all ingredients except collards to a pot over low heat; simmer 1 hour. Add collards; cover and simmer 2 more hours, or until tender.

Restaurant Recipe

Mac and Cheese

Mac and Cheese is an On Forty-One favorite.

2 teaspoons chopped shallots
2 teaspoons chopped garlic
½ quart heavy cream
½ quart half-and-half
3 ounces cream cheese
Slurry for thickening (4 tablespoons each flour and water, mixed)
3 slices American cheese
2 cups Parmesan cheese
6 ounces Fontina cheese
6 ounces shredded sharp Cheddar cheese plus more for topping
Salt and pepper to taste
5 pounds elbow noodles, cooked according to package directions

Preheat oven to 350°. Lightly sweat shallots and garlic in a saucepan over medium-low heat. Add cream and half-and-half and heat; stir in cream cheese until melted. Add slurry to thicken mixture as needed. Remove from heat and add remaining cheeses; blend with hand blender and strain. Stir in elbow noodles and transfer to a buttered casserole dish. Top with additional Cheddar cheese. Bake 20 minutes uncovered.

Restaurant Recipe

PITT ST. PHARMACY
DRUGS
Compounding Since 1937

Pitt Street Pharmacy Soda Fountain

111 Pitt Street
Mount Pleasant, SC 29464
843-884-4051
www.pittstreetpharmacy.com • **Find us on Facebook**

Pitt Street Pharmacy has been serving Mount Pleasant for more than eighty years. This compounding pharmacy specializes in serving its customers' unique needs. It is also home to the Soda Fountain, a diner-style attachment featuring delicious food, ice cream, milkshakes, and fountain drinks. Stop by for a grilled cheese, Mrs. Linda's famous egg salad sandwich, ice cream floats, malts, and more. The diner even carries a wonderful selection of gifts. The Soda Fountain is a place where generations have grown up, memories are made, and even movies have been filmed. Local, tourist, or celebrity—everyone feels at home at the Pitt Street Pharmacy Soda Fountain. Come in, relax, and enjoy.

Monday – Saturday: 9:00 am to 6:00 pm

Pimento Cheese

1 (4-ounce) block New York sharp Cheddar cheese

1 (4-ounce) jar pimentos with juice, finely mashed

1 cup Duke's mayonnaise

1 medium onion, finely grated

Salt and pepper to taste

Dash sugar

4 dashes Texas Pete hot sauce

1 tablespoon Worcestershire sauce

Leave cheese out overnight to soften in package. In a large bowl, grate cheese with a hand grater. Add remaining ingredients and mix until well combined. Serve on white or wheat bread, plain or toasted.

Restaurant Recipe

The "Bosie" Tuna Salad

The "Bosie" Tuna Salad was named after Betty Rose "Bosie" Carter. She came in every Thursday afternoon to get her tuna salad sandwich for more than 25 years until her passing in 2017. It was named the "Bosie" because anyone at the soda fountain counter knew when she walked in the door what she wanted.

2 (12-ounce) cans tuna in water, drained

½ cup diced celery

2 hard-boiled egg whites, chopped

¾ cup Duke's mayonnaise

Salt and pepper to taste

In a large bowl, mix all ingredients until well combined. Serve on a bed of lettuce or as a sandwich made with white or wheat bread, plain or toasted.

Restaurant Recipe

ARE YOU THIRSTY? VERY, VERY THIRSTY?

The world's largest sweet tea is 2,254 gallons, in a mason jar standing 15 feet tall. When traveling through Summerville, you can stop anytime—day or night—to visit "Mason" in the courtyard at the Town of Summerville Municipal Complex.

Brewing this gigantic glass of tea required 210 pounds of local tea from the Charleston Tea Plantation and 1,700 pounds of sugar. This world record was verified by Guinness World Records. The official record shows that organizers originally used 300 pounds of ice to chill the tea. When that didn't cool the warm tea to the required 45 degrees, several hundred additional pounds of ice were added.

The world record was achieved by Summerville for the second time on June 10, 2016—National Iced Tea Day. The World's Largest Iced Tea record was first held by Chick-fil-A for 912 gallons in 2010, before Summerville took the record in 2015 with 1,452 gallons. A few months later, Lipton took the title with a 2,204-gallon display.

Obviously, Summerville doesn't give up easily, as the world record is home again in The Birthplace of Sweet Tea.

Sweet Life

SUMMERVILLE, SC

Town of Summerville Municipal Complex

200 South Main Street
Summerville, SC 29483
843-871-6000
www.visitsummerville.com

While you are there, check out:

Charleston Tea Plantation
www.charlestonteaplantation.com

Water's Edge Restaurant

**1407 Shrimp Boat Lane
Mount Pleasant, SC 29464
843-884-4074
www.waters-edge-restaurant.com
Find us on Facebook**

Located on scenic Shem Creek just minutes from historic Downtown Charleston, Water's Edge offers both waterfront and outdoor dining. Guests can enjoy their meals while watching local fish and shrimp boats unload their daily catches. The creative chefs at Water's Edge have fashioned a menu that appeals to every taste by featuring fresh local fish, prime rib, and many more Lowcountry dishes. The wine list proudly boast over 450 selections of affordably priced wines from around the world. Stop in for happy hour and enjoy a glass of wine with a delicious meal inspired by Lowcountry tradition.

Daily: 11:00 am until

She-Crab Soup

½ stick butter
¼ cup chopped white onion
¼ cup chopped celery
½ cup flour
1 tablespoon freshly chopped parsley
1 teaspoon freshly chopped thyme
1 teaspoon ground mace
Salt and pepper to taste
1 teaspoon Florida Bay seasoning
2 tablespoons sherry
1 cup milk
½ cup heavy cream
¼ cup blue crab claw meat

In a saucepan over medium heat, melt butter; add onion and celery and stir to coat. Place lid on saucepan and sweat 10 to 15 minutes, stirring occasionally, until onion is translucent. Stir in dry ingredients; cook 10 to 12 minutes, stirring frequently. Add sherry; cook 5 minutes. Slowly add milk and cream while stirring. Continue cooking over medium-low heat until desired consistency is reach. Fold in crabmeat.

Restaurant Recipe

Seafood Paella

Paella Broth:

Dash oil
¼ cup chopped red onion
¼ cup chopped celery
1 teaspoon Florida Bay seasoning
Splash Worcestershire sauce
Pinch saffron
1 teaspoon sugar
1 tablespoon tomato paste
1 cup chopped tomato

In a large saucepan over medium heat, add oil, onion and celery; place lid on pan and sweat vegetables 10 to 15 minutes, stirring occasionally. Stir in Florida Bay, Worcestershire, saffron and sugar. Stir in tomato paste, tomato and 1½ cups water. Bring to a boil, then remove from heat and set aside to cool.

4 large shrimp, peeled and deveined
4 scallops
4 clams, shelled
4 mussels, shelled
4 whitefish fillets
1 (4-ounce) Maine lobster tail, split
1 teaspoon chopped shallots
1 teaspoon chopped garlic
Salt and pepper to taste
Splash white wine
Freshly chopped basil and chives for garnish
1 cup prepared saffron rice

In a medium skillet over medium-low heat, sauté seafood until almost done cooking. Add shallots, garlic, salt, pepper, wine and 1½ cups prepared Paella Broth. Garnish with basil and chives. Serve over saffron rice.

Restaurant Recipe

LoLA

4830 O'Hear Avenue
North Charleston, SC 29405
843-990-9416
www.lolaparkcircle.com • Find us on Facebook

LoLA started as a food truck in 2010, eventually opening its brick-and-mortar location in 2016. This charming restaurant features Louisiana-style cuisine in a Lowcountry, family-friendly atmosphere. Find savory dishes like overstuffed po-boys, perfectly seasoned crawfish and oysters, flavorful gumbo, and lots of other Cajun pub fare and great dinner specials each night. Visit LoLA for happy hour, Tuesday through Friday, when you will enjoy great discounts on food and drinks. The outside patio is pet friendly, so your furry friends are also welcome. Drop by LoLA for friendly service and some of the best Louisiana-style cuisine available in North Charleston. On- and off-premise catering is also available.

Tuesday – Thursday: 11:00 am to 9:00 pm
Friday & Saturday: 11:00 am to 9:30 pm

Salmon Alexander

Cajun Cream Sauce:

½ stick butter
1 shallot, minced
2 cloves garlic, minced
2 cups heavy cream
2 tablespoons Cajun paste

In a saucepan over medium heat, melt butter. Sauté shallot and garlic 1 minute or until translucent. Stir in cream and Cajun paste. Reduce by half, stirring occasionally, until cream thickens.

¾ pound sea scallops, cut in half
12 ounces shrimp, peeled and deveined
12 ounces crawfish tail meat
Oil and butter as needed
2¼ pounds Atlantic salmon, skinned and cut into 6-ounce fillets
Blackening spices to taste
Prepared stone-ground grits
Sliced green onions for garnish

In a saucepan over medium heat, sauté scallops and shrimp until medium rare, about 2 minutes. Add crawfish; cook 2 minutes more. Add prepared Cajun Cream Sauce; toss. Heat until cream mixture bubbles, then set aside, covered if necessary. In a cast-iron skillet over medium-high heat, add oil and butter. Add salmon; blacken with blackening spices to your liking to medium doneness; set aside. To assemble, plate grits in a 10-inch bowl. Center a salmon fillet on grits and ladle seafood in Cajun Cream Sauce over top. Garnish with green onion.

Restaurant Recipe

Shrimp Creole

Creole Sauce:

2 sticks butter
8 cups finely diced onion
2 cups finely diced celery
2 cups finely diced green bell pepper
8 tablespoons Creole seasoning, divided
¼ cup minced garlic
4 pounds Creole tomatoes, chopped
8 cups vegetable stock
40 ounces tomato puree
4 to 5 bay leaves
3 tablespoons sugar
Tabasco to taste
¼ cup Worcestershire
1 lemon, halved and deseeded

In a large stockpot over medium heat, melt butter. Sauté onion, celery and bell pepper 5 minutes. Add half seasoning; cook 10 minutes or until vegetables are translucent. Add garlic, tomatoes and remaining seasoning; cook 10 minutes. Stir in stock and puree. Grind with an immersion blender if a smooth texture is desired. Stir in remaining ingredients, and reduce heat; simmer 30 minutes. Discard lemon and bay leaves.

⅓ pound shrimp per person
Oil and butter as needed
4 tablespoons Creole seasoning
Prepared long-grain rice or stone-ground grits
Toasted, sliced French bread

In a large stockpot over medium-high heat, sauté shrimp in oil, butter and seasoning 2 minutes. Add prepared Creole Sauce and toss. Serve over rice or grits with French bread to soak up the goodness.

Restaurant Recipe

Nigel's Good Food

3760 Ashley Phosphate Road
North Charleston, SC 29418
843-552-0079

9616 Highway 78, Suite 11
Ladson, SC 29456
843-718-1759
www.nigelsgoodfood.com • Facebook.com/nigelsgoodfood

Nigel's Good Food is owned by Nigel and Louise Drayton and operated by a team with great passion for serving and satisfying their guests. Chef Nigel Drayton grew up on authentic, Charleston-style soul food and seafood. Now he brings those traditional flavors to you in every dish he prepares. Nigel's boasts an extensive menu and a full bar with daily happy hour specials. Locals love the Geechie wings served with blue cheese vinaigrette dressing. The team at Nigel's strives to provide the best experience to each guest every time they visit. Drop by Nigel's Good Food for a dining experience that's just what your soul needs.

Monday – Thursday: 11:00 am to 10:00 pm
Friday & Saturday: 11:00 am to 11:00 pm

Lowcountry Ravioli with Whiskey Butter

Whiskey Butter:

1 pound butter, softened
½ cup whiskey
¼ cup minced red onions
6 tablespoons Cajun seasoning

In a bowl, mix together all ingredients until well-combined; set aside.

Ravioli:

1 (7-ounce) chicken breast, grilled and chopped
3 to 4 slices bacon, cooked and crumbled
½ cup cooked collard greens
¼ cup cooked black-eyed peas
¼ cup cooked corn kernels
1½ cups heavy cream
5 pieces frozen cheese-stuffed ravioli
Salt, pepper and garlic powder to taste
1 ounce grated Parmesan cheese, plus more for garnish

In a skillet over medium heat, sauté chicken, bacon, collards, black-eyed peas and corn 6 to 8 minutes. Stir in heavy cream. Add ravioli, salt, pepper and garlic powder. Cook 8 to 10 minutes, stirring occasionally, until thickened. Stir in 1 ounce Parmesan and 1 tablespoon Whiskey Butter. Ladle Ravioli into a bowl and garnish with extra Parmesan. Enjoy.

Restaurant Recipe

Old-Fashioned Banana Pudding

5 to 6 bananas, sliced
1 (10-ounce) package vanilla wafers
1¾ cups sugar, divided
¼ cup flour
4 eggs, separated
2 cups milk
1 (12-ounce) can evaporated milk
Dash salt
1 teaspoon vanilla
½ teaspoon cream of tartar

Using 2 (9-inch) loaf pans, layer banana slices and wafers. In a double boiler, mix 1 cup sugar, flour and egg yolks. Add milks, salt and vanilla; stir well. Place mixture over boiling water, stirring constantly until thickened. Pour over bananas and wafers. Using an electric mixer, beat egg whites and cream of tartar, while slowly adding remaining sugar, until stiff peaks form. Spread this meringue over each pudding being sure it completely covers from edge to edge. Place under oven broiler until browned.

Local Favorite

Rice Casserole

1 stick margarine
1 cup uncooked rice
½ cup chopped onion
½ cup chopped celery
1 (10.75-ounce) can cream of onion soup
1 (14-ounce) can beef broth

Preheat oven to 375°. In a skillet, melt butter. Add rice, onions and celery; cook until rice is slightly brown, about 3 minutes. Pour into a 9x9-inch casserole dish; stir in onion soup and beef broth. Cover and bake 1 hour.

Local Favorite

Ham Bone Dumplings

1 large ham bone (or cubed leftover ham)
1 teaspoon salt, plus more for stock
Pepper to taste
2½ cups flour
½ cup Crisco shortening
1 cup ice cold water

Simmer ham bone in a Dutch oven with 2 quarts water for 20 minutes. Taste and add salt and pepper if needed. Using a large bowl, combine flour and 1 teaspoon salt; cut in shortening until crumbly. Add ice water and mix to form dough. Add more flour, if needed, to make dough easy to handle. Roll out dough very thin on floured surface. Cut dough into thin strips and drop by small pieces into broth. Cook 20 to 25 minutes. Turn off heat and let rest 5 minutes before serving.

Local Favorite

Pecan Fig Pie

1 cup chopped pecans
3 cups peeled figs
2 tablespoons lemon juice
½ cup brown sugar
¼ cup flour
1 (9-inch) deep-dish pie crust
¼ cup cold butter
1 (9-inch) ready-to-bake pie crust
1 egg
3 tablespoons sugar

Preheat oven to 350°. In a large bowl, mix pecans, figs, lemon juice, brown sugar and flour; refrigerate 30 minutes. Bake deep-dish pie 12 minutes or until just slightly brown. Pour pecan mixture in pie shell and cover with pats of butter. Place 2nd pie crust over top and crimp edges with fork. Trim excess dough around edges and cut 4 diagonal slits in top. Beat egg in small bowl with ½ tablespoon water. Using a pastry brush, brush egg over top of pie. Sprinkle with sugar. Bake 20 minutes. If top is not brown enough, place under broiler until brown, taking care not to burn pie.

Local Favorite

Shug's Southern Soul Café

5792 Memorial Boulevard
Saint George, SC 29477
843-563-2300
www.shugssouthernsoulcafe.com • Find us on Facebook

Opened in 2006 in Ridgeville, in a town called Pringletown, Shug's Southern Soul Café specializes in Southern and American food. Owners Noah and Blanche Coleman named the restaurant after Shug Avery, the fictional jazz and blues singer from *The Color Purple*. Shug's has since moved to Saint George and still serves up that special soul food and hospitality for which it is known. Guests can chow down on classics like shrimp and grits, collards, red rice, fried chicken, seafood, steaks, pasta, burgers, and ribs. Swing by Shug's Southern Soul Café today for good food, family, and entertainment.

Wednesday & Thursday: 11:00 am to 9:00 pm
Friday & Saturday: 11:00 am to 10:00 pm
Sunday: 11:00 am to 4:00 pm

shuga
Southern Soul Café

Shug's She-Crab Soup

1 cup butter
1 cup finely chopped carrots
1 cup finely chopped celery
4 tablespoons flour
2 quarts heavy cream
2 quarts whole milk
Old Bay Seasoning to taste
Salt and pepper to taste
1½ to 2 pounds crab claws or crabmeat
Sherry to taste

Using a Dutch oven over medium heat, melt butter. Add carrots and celery; sauté until tender. Add flour; stirring constantly, cook until light brown. Slowly add heavy cream and milk, mixing thoroughly to prevent lumps. Add seasonings. Reduce heat to medium low and cook, stirring occasionally, until sauce begins to thicken. Stir in crab and a touch of sherry. Cook an additional 5 minutes.

Restaurant Recipe

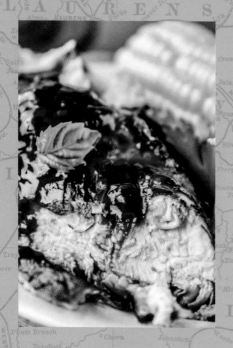

Time Well Spent Tea Room

211 Stallsville Loop
Summerville, SC 29485
843-875-2408
www.theperfectpartyplace.info • Find us on Facebook

Nestled under a 900-year-old oak tree in the Flowertown area of Summerville, Time Well Spent Tea Room has made its home. This family-owned, quaint, Victorian-style tea room has been serving the Summerville area for over twenty-five years. Decorated with classic Victorian touches and whimsical flair, Time Well Spent is perfect for lunch with friends, afternoon tea, or a range of special events from weddings to birthday parties. Guests will enjoy freshly made, home-style meals in a relaxing atmosphere. Visit Time Well Spent Tea Room soon, as time with friends and family is time well spent.

Lunch:
Tuesday – Saturday: 11:00 am to 2:30 pm
Afternoon Tea (Reservation Only):
Thursday – Saturday: 2:30 pm to 4:30 pm

Sandles She-Crab Soup

5 tablespoons flour
5 tablespoons butter
1 small onion, grated
1 stalk celery, grated
2 cloves garlic, minced
Salt and pepper to taste
2 quarts half-and-half
1 cup lobster stock
1 pint heavy cream
½ cup sherry wine, divided
Chopped dill to taste
2 teaspoons Worcestershire sauce
1 teaspoon hot sauce
1 pound lump crabmeat
2 tablespoons chopped chives

In a saucepan over medium heat, add flour and butter to make a roux; cook about 3 minutes, stirring constantly. Mix in onion, celery, garlic, salt and pepper; cook about 4 minutes. Whisk in half-and-half, then stock and cream. Bring to a simmer. Add ¼ cup sherry. Add dill, Worcestershire and hot sauce. Cover and simmer about 10 minutes. Remove from heat, cool and gently fold in crabmeat. Serve with a garnish of chives and a splash of remaining sherry wine over top.

Restaurant Recipe

ABANDONED TOWN, ARCHEOLOGICAL SITE OR STATE PARK?

The town of Dorchester—the third settlement in South Carolina—is an historic site situated on a neck of land between the Ashley River and Dorchester Creek, originally known as Boshoe Creek. It was colonized by a group of Puritans who resettled from Dorchester, Massachusetts, to this site on the upper Ashley River in 1696.

They first built a church in the center of what would become Dorchester. St. George's Anglican Church was completed in 1719 and the bell tower, which stands today, was added in 1751.

Dorchester was laid out in an orderly fashion, with 116 quarter-acre lots between parallel and perpendicular streets. The main thoroughfare was called High Street, as was traditionally done in small British towns. They left an open area in the town for a marketplace.

The site's advantageous location helped the town thrive. Nearby roads led to Charleston, and the Ashley River provided a convenient highway for the shipment of goods and produce. Trade with Native Americans, the development of rice and indigo as cash crops, and a growing population helped secure Dorchester's economic peak in the mid-1700s. A biweekly market was established in 1723 and a Free School dedicated in 1734. By 1781, Dorchester additionally boasted about forty houses, a library, and a fort overlooking a strategic bend in the river. Fifty-acre farm lots lined the riverbank, and there was a wharf, boat-building facilities, and a bridge across the Ashley. By 1748, the town's population was almost four thousand.

Dorchester's location made it a strategic military site. Fear of a possible French invasion prompted the construction of a powder magazine and fort from 1757 to 1760. Originally designed to be constructed using brick, the fort and powder magazine were eventually made of tabby, a concrete material made of lime, sand, and oyster shells. The wall is eight feet at its highest and two feet to two feet ten inches at the bottom. It encloses a rectangular area of more than 10,000 square feet. During the Revolutionary War, the fort was a rendezvous point for local militia units. The fort fell to the British when Charles Town fell in 1780. The British held the fort until 1781, then left, burning the town and driving away most of its remaining residents.

After the war, the fort housed a tile yard, with the magazine converted into a kiln for firing clay roofing tiles. But like the rest of town, the fort was soon abandoned. By the early 1800s, little remained of the formerly bustling town but ruins of homes, their bricks scavenged for reuse in nearby Summerville. The Great Charleston Earthquake of 1886, whose epicenter was less than a mile from Dorchester, destroyed the ruins, except for the old church tower, its graveyard, and the walls of the fort. The site was covered by brush and trees until the Colonial Dames of America cleared the brush in the 1920s.

In 1969, the site was donated to the South Carolina State Park Service and was added to the National Register of Historic Places. Today, the property is the site of a 325-acre park where you can stand below the towering remains of the brick bell tower of St. George's Anglican Church, catch a glimpse of a log wharf during low tide, or view one of the most well-preserved oyster-shell tabby forts in the country.

Colonial Dorchester State Historic Site offers you a glimpse into South Carolina's colonial past, with burial sites and cemeteries as well as ongoing archaeological digs that are still unearthing the settlement's history. An interpretive trail with kiosks and exhibits explains the history of the village that once prospered here.

Colonial Dorchester State Historic Site

300 State Park Road
Summerville, SC 29485
843-873-1740
www.southcarolinaparks.com/colonial-dorchester

Low Country Seafood

204 East Carolina Avenue
Varnville, SC 29944
803-943-0170

Looking for the perfect place to end your long day? Look no further. The Low Country Seafood restaurant will welcome you with its friendly service and aromatic kitchen. Located in the heart of Varnville, Low Country Seafood should not be missed. Stop by today for rib-eye steaks, lobster, shrimp, scallops, oysters, and more.

Monday – Saturday: 11:00 am to 9:00 pm
Sunday: 11:00 am to 3:00 pm

Potato Casserole

6 large potatoes
1 stick butter
**2 cups grated sharp Cheddar
cheese, divided**
2 cups sour cream
1 cup milk
⅔ cup chopped onions

Boil potatoes in jackets; chill until cold and shred with grater. Melt butter in double boiler. Stir in cheese gradually, reserving ½ cup. In a bowl, mix together sour cream and milk; add to cheese mixture. Add onions. Transfer to a treated 9x13-inch baking dish and bake at 350° for 40 minutes. Remove from oven and sprinkle remaining cheese over top; bake an additional 5 minutes, or until cheese is melted. Serves 8 to 10.

Local Favorite

Rice Waffles

1 cup flour
1 teaspoon baking powder
1 cup cold cooked rice
1 tablespoon melted butter
½ teaspoon salt
3 eggs, beaten

Preheat and grease waffle iron. In a bowl, sift together flour and baking powder. Add rice, butter, salt and eggs. Using back of a spoon, mash rice very fine into other ingredients; mix well. Pour batter into iron and cook until golden brown.

Local Favorite

Hamburger Steak

12 ounces lean ground beef
Salt and pepper to taste
½ medium onion, sliced
1 tablespoon vegetable oil
2 tablespoons flour
1 cup beef broth

Season meat with salt and pepper. Form into a patty. In a skillet or on a flat grill, cook patty about 4 minutes on each side, or until cooked to your satisfaction; remove from heat. Grill onions until golden brown; set aside. In a skillet over medium-high heat, add oil. Add flour and stir with a fork. Season with more salt and pepper, mixing well; cook until medium brown. Slowly add broth while constantly stirring. Reduce heat and simmer 5 minutes, stirring occasionally, until gravy thickens. Plate patty; top with onions and gravy. Enjoy.

Local Favorite

New Potato Poppers

Oil for frying
Salt
16 to 20 quarter-size new potatoes

Wash potatoes thoroughly. Leave skins on or remove, your choice. Place potatoes in a saucepan, cover with salted water and boil until fork tender. Drain on paper towels until completely dry. Heat oil in deep fryer to 325°. Place potatoes in basket and slowly lower into oil. Fry 6 minutes. Remove from oil and drain. Makes a wonderful side dish to any meat entrée.

Local Favorite

Breakfast Pizza

1 pound pork sausage
1 (8-ounce) package crescent rolls
1 cup shredded hash browns, thawed
**1 (8-ounce) package shredded sharp
Cheddar cheese**
3 eggs
¼ cup milk
½ teaspoon salt
⅛ teaspoon pepper
2 tablespoons grated Parmesan cheese

Preheat oven to 375°. In a skillet over medium-high heat, brown sausage; drain and set aside. Separate crescent dough into 8 triangles; place on an ungreased 12-inch pizza pan with triangle points toward center. Press side seams of triangles together to make a pizza crust. Spoon sausage over crust and sprinkle on potatoes; top with cheese. In a bowl, beat eggs with milk, salt and pepper; pour over sausage. Sprinkle with Parmesan. Bake 25 to 30 minutes.

Local Favorite

Quick Chicken & Rice Soup

3 (14.5-ounce) cans chicken broth
1½ cups quick-cooking rice
**1 pound skinless, boneless chicken
breasts, cut into ½-inch cubes**
1½ teaspoons minced fresh ginger
1 tablespoon hot chili oil
1 tablespoon rice wine vinegar
1 bunch scallions, thinly sliced

In a large saucepan over high heat, bring chicken broth, rice and 3 cups water to a boil. Add chicken; reduce heat to medium low. Cover and cook about 6 minutes, or until rice is tender and chicken is white in center. Add ginger, chili oil, vinegar and scallions; cook 2 minutes more to blend flavors. Enjoy.

Local Favorite

Olde House Cafe

1274 Bells Highway
Walterboro, SC 29488
843-538-2614

Olde House Cafe's motto is "Country Cookin' makes you good lookin.'" You'll find all the country cooking you could ever dream of at Olde House. This simple diner serves down-home American fare like seafood platters, rib-eyes, and country breakfasts. Sample savory hamburger steaks, fried pork chops, grilled chicken breasts, fried flounder, fried shrimp, fried catfish fillets, and more.

Monday – Saturday: 6:30 am to 9:00 pm
Sunday: 6:30 am to 3:00 pm

Potato Casserole

2 pounds frozen diced potatoes
1 (10.5-ounce) can cream of chicken and
mushroom soup
1¼ cups sour cream
1 stick butter, melted
1 cup grated American cheese
1 cup grated Cheddar cheese
Salt and pepper to taste
French's Original crispy fried
onions, optional
Corn flakes cereal, optional

Mix casserole ingredients together in a bowl. Bake at 350° for 45 minutes to 1 hour or until browned. If desired, sprinkle top with fried onions or corn flakes the last 5 minutes of baking.

Restaurant Recipe

Catfish Stew

15 pounds catfish fillets
2 (28-ounce) cans diced tomatoes
15 pounds potatoes, diced
5 pounds bacon, diced
8 pounds onions, diced
3 quarts ketchup
Salt and pepper to taste

In a 10-gallon stockpot over high heat, add catfish and enough water to cover. Add tomatoes (with juice) and boil until catfish is done; remove from heat. In a separate large stockpot over high heat, boil potatoes until soft. Meanwhile, fry bacon in a skillet over medium heat until crispy; drain on paper towels. Add onions to skillet and fry in bacon drippings until translucent; drain on paper towels and discard bacon drippings. Add potatoes, bacon and onions to pot with catfish. Stir in ketchup. Season with salt and pepper. Add enough water to cover by 6 inches and simmer over low heat until cooked down.

Restaurant Recipe

RESTAURANT INDEX

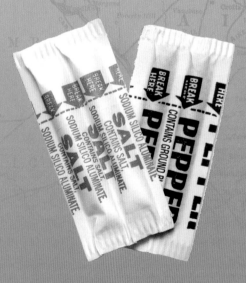

RECIPE INDEX

C

More Great American Books

NEW

My Notebook Series
Alabama • Georgia • Mississippi
Retail $14.95 • Wire-O-bound • 5⅜ x 8¼ • 192 pages

Farm to Table Fabulous is a back-to-basics approach to cooking and entertaining. This easy-to-follow cookbook will guide you through the seasons with 12 monthly menus for preparing delicious step-by-step meals and tips for hosting a dinner party any month of the year. Using the freshest ingredients for cooking and decorating, you'll create a casual yet enchanting experience for your guests... one they will talk about for years to come.

Farm to Table Fabulous
$18.95 • 256 pages • 7x10
paperbound • full color

Church Recipes are the Best

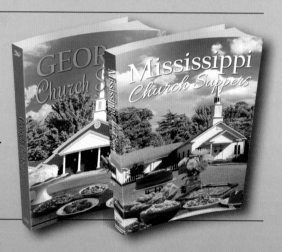

Georgia Church Suppers
$18.95 • 256 pages • 7x10 • paperbound • full color

Mississippi Church Suppers
$21.95 • 288 pages • 7x10 • paperbound • full color

Little Gulf Coast Seafood Cookbook
$14.95 • 192 pages • 5½x8½
paperbound • full color

Game for all Seasons Cookbook
$16.95 • 240 pages • 7x10
paperbound • full color

The Ultimate Venison Cookbook for Deer Camp
$21.95 • 288 pages • 7x10
paperbound • full color

Kids in the Kitchen
$18.95 • 256 pages
7x10 • paperbound • full color

Great American Grilling
$21.95 • 288 pages • 7x10
paperbound • full color

Betty B's Having a Party!
A Holiday Dinner
Party Cookbook
$18.95 • 256 pages • 7x9
paperbound • full color

State Hometown Cookbook Series
A Hometown Taste of America, One State at a Time.

EACH: $18.95 • 240 to 272 pages • 7x10 • paperbound

Alabama • Georgia • Louisiana • Mississippi
South Carolina • Tennessee • Texas • West Virginia

Eat & Explore Cookbook Series
Discover community celebrations and unique destinations, as they share their favorite recipes.

EACH: $18.95 • 240 to 272 pages • 7x9 • paperbound

Arkansas • Illinois • Minnesota • North Carolina
Ohio • Oklahoma • Virginia • Washington

www.GreatAmericanPublishers.com • www.facebook.com/GreatAmericanPublishers

State Back Road Restaurants Series

From two-lane highways and interstates, to dirt roads and quaint downtowns, every road leads to delicious food when traveling across our United States. The STATE BACK ROAD RESTAURANTS COOKBOOK SERIES serves up a well-researched and charming guide to each state's best back road restaurants. No time to travel? No problem. Each restaurant shares with you their favorite recipes—sometimes their signature dish, sometimes a family favorite, but always delicious.

EACH: $18.95 • 256 pages • 7x9 • paperbound • full-color

Alabama • Kentucky • Louisiana • Missouri • North Carolina
South Carolina • Tennessee • Texas

3 Easy Ways to Order

1) Call toll-free **1-888-854-5954** to order by phone or to request a free catalog.

2) Order online at **www.GreatAmericanPublishers.com**

3) Mail a check or money order for the cost of the book(s) plus $5 shipping for the first book and $1 each additional plus a list of the books you want to order along with your name, address, phone and email to:

Great American Publishers
171 Lone Pine Church Road
Lena MS 39094

Find us on facebook: www.facebook.com/GreatAmericanPublishers

Join the We Love 2 Cook Club and get a 10% discount.
www.GreatAmericanPublishers.com